What Readers Are Saying About *His Revolutionary Love: Jesus' Radical Pursuit of You*

I'm making this book a must-read for each of my teen daughters. Lynn knows how to connect with the heart of today's teen girls and unpack the real issues in a relevant, fun way. I give this book my highest recommendation for moms and daughters alike!

—Lysa TerKeurst, *New York Times* best-selling author of *Made to Crave* and mom to five priority blessings

The most amazing love story in the world is the one between you and God. Entering inside this love story will bring fulfillment, confidence, healthy self-esteem, and true joy! Lynn Cowell guides teen girls into the greatest love story of their lives through diary entries, interactive experiences, fiction scenarios, and real-life examples. *His Revolutionary Love* isn't simply a "read," it's an *experience*. It's totally fun . . . yet life-changing at the same time!

—Susie Shellenberger, editor, *SUSIE Magazine*

Do you want to be a girl with confidence? . . . If so, you've picked up the right book. I believe as you read *His Revolutionary Love,* you'll see a side of Jesus that you may have never seen before.

—From the foreword by Brenda Warner, coauthor of *First Things First* with husband and Super Bowl-winning quarterback Kurt Warner

His Revolutionary Love is a really good book that teaches girls like me that we can go to God for anything because he is there for us every day and every night. It also teaches us about his extraordinary love for us. I personally liked all of Lynn Cowell's diary entries. Overall, I had a great experience with this book.

—Cailee Ketter, 11, Pennsylvania

If you have a heart for seeing young girls be drawn into the love of Jesus, listen up. Using *His Revolutionary Love,* I led a Bible study for a small group of girls from ages nine to thirteen. I loved seeing how it spoke to them all in a unique way. This book captures Jesus' pursuit of us in such a way that these girls really were able to take hold of that truth and let it take root. Lynn did a fabulous job sharing the heart of a Savior who is longing for us to realize just how great his love is and gently leads us to respond to that radical love!

—Brittany Lee Ketter, 19, college student, Pennsylvania

When I first read about *His Revolutior   to not just read it but *soak it in*. I felt like God w   the teen girl's wounded spirit within me. As a   nd want to help her avoid making the same mi   a teen. I want to help guide my daughter close   y love for her. Lynn's book is helping me do just

—Erin Bishop, founder and ministry director, the Whatever Girls, Spokane, Washington

There are so many things I love about Lynn Cowell. She's fun, energetic, and has a passion for Jesus and teen girls. In *His Revolutionary Love* she clearly explains that Jesus is the answer to every question girls are asking. The love of Jesus truly does change everything—and this book will change you.

—Shannon Primicerio, author of *The Divine Dance*, *God Called a Girl*, and the True Life Bible study series

I lead two discipleship groups of teen girls, so I'm always looking for great resources. I can confidently say this book is a gem. Biblically sound, balanced with stories, this resource will be the next one I grab when I lead my girls. I love the central message of this book—that girls are wildly loved by Jesus. Such a needed truth in today's crazy world!

—Mary DeMuth, author of *Thin Places: A Memoir* and *A Slow Burn*

His Revolutionary Love is an incredible message to young girls that their identity can be found only in Jesus—not in any man. Lynn reminds us that if you come to realize this truth, you'll find an unconditional love and a consuming fire for the Lord that can never be quenched.

—Jamie Waldron, student director at Elevation Church, Matthews, North Carolina

I have received much conviction concerning my walk with Christ. For so long I've struggled with consistency. Please continue to share the truth of *His Revolutionary Love* with girls. This is coming from a 20-year-old single college kid who was emancipated. A girl who struggled with depression, self-hatred, eating disorders, alcohol, drugs, lust, thoughts of suicide, and the comprehension of never feeling loved. . . . But praise Jesus—he is bigger and has rescued me!

— Amber, 20, Louisiana

Being in Lynn's group and receiving this teaching was a godsend! It really made me aware of a deeper level that I could go to with my Savior, a relationship where I am his cherished daughter who is dearly loved. This teaching also helped me realize that I don't need to fall under the pressures of boys, peers, or our cultural norms to be accepted and loved. Just by reaching out to Jesus, I can see that he takes care of all my needs, all my worries and insecurities, and all my pains and heartbreaks. Through this teaching, I ultimately learned that he accepts me exactly the way I am.

—Laurli Pleiman, 21, North Carolina

His Revolutionary Love

Jesus' Radical Pursuit of You

LYNN COWELL

Standard PUBLISHING

Cincinnati, Ohio

Published by Standard Publishing, Cincinnati, Ohio
www.standardpub.com

Printed in: United States of America
Acquisitions editor: Robert Irvin
Project editor: Laura Derico
Cover design: Jenette McEntire
Interior design: Jenette McEntire, Scott Ryan

While all of the stories and quotations in this book noted as coming from teens (or former teens)
are true, in some instances names and details have been changed in order to protect the identities
of those involved.

Published in association with the literary agency of The Blythe Daniel Agency Inc., PO Box
64197, Colorado Springs, CO 80962-4197.

ISBN 978-0-7847-2981-6

Library of Congress Cataloging-in-Publication Data

Cowell, Lynn, 1967-
  His revolutionary love : Jesus' radical pursuit of you / Lynn Cowell.
    p. cm.
  Includes bibliographical references (p.   ).
  ISBN 978-0-7847-2981-6
  1. Teenage girls--Religious life. 2. Christian girls--Religious life. 3. Love--Religious aspects--
Christianity. I. Title.
  BV4551.3C69 2011
  248.8'33--dc22
                              2010053565

16 15 14 13 12 11   2 3 4 5 6 7 8 9

TO GREG

*Thank you for always believing in me and
loving me selflessly, like Christ.*

Contents

That Much?

When I was growing up, in our house love was everything. My mom and dad were so affectionate; I just thought that's how everyone's family was. In fact, I didn't know any different until Lynn came over. She would ask questions like, "Why do your parents snuggle together on the couch?" "How come your parents are always smooching?"

That love spilled over to my sister, Kim, and me as well. We always had to kiss our parents when we left the house, even if it was only to go across the street! I really grew to depend on that love. Then my parents both died in a tornado. I am so glad that Jesus' love was already in place in my life before that happened.

I experienced his love for me just before middle school; the "revolutionary" side of it appealed to me most of all. Even in high school I thrived on being bold about my faith. Lynn and I were known in our high school as "Jesus freaks." We loved him and wanted others to know the power of this awesome God.

WHEN LIFE WAS HARD, HE WAS THE ONE THING THAT WAS CONSTANT—THE ONE THING I COULD COUNT ON.

That love, in high school and when my parents died, gave me exactly what I needed. Strength. Boldness. Tenacity. The power to live a meaningful life—using my gifts and talents to tell others of his amazing love, even when my own experiences have been less than perfect. When life was hard, he was the one thing that was constant—the one thing I could count on.

Jesus' radical love has made all the difference in my life and I know it will in my future too. Good things in this life come and go. I know—I've been on both sides. I have been rich; I've been poor. Looks, fame, money, even friendships and (unfortunately) family change, but Jesus' love never does. That is why we need it; that's why we need so much to be filled with him. We need a love that is secure, never wavers, and is stronger than the strongest storm.

Do you want to be a girl with confidence? a girl who shines no matter if she is popular today but not tomorrow? a girl so filled with the truth that Jesus is wild about her that she can't help but influence those who are around her? If so, you've picked up the right book. I believe as you read *His Revolutionary Love* you'll see a side of Jesus that you may have never seen before. I believe that, just as he fills every part of my heart and gives my life purpose and value, he will do the same for you as you run after him.

Brenda Warner is the coauthor of *First Things First: The Rules of Being a Warner,* with husband, Kurt Warner, Super Bowl champion quarterback.

The Love Story Begins

Call it a crush. Say he was hot. It doesn't really matter how you word it. I liked him; he didn't like me.

It's not like I wanted to be the most popular, the most beautiful, or even the smartest. I just wanted to be wanted. Was that asking too much? If all this guy stuff was supposed to be such a great thing, then why was my crush crushing me?

Have you ever been there? On the wrong end of a love equation? Guy + Me = Value? *I* simply was never part of that math problem. I had been told I was cute, fun to be around, a good friend. Then what was wrong with me?

The truth was . . . nothing! Absolutely nothing! There was and is nothing wrong with me—just like there is nothing wrong with you. We have always been loved in an extraordinary way; we've just missed the love that has been loving us all along.

PLASTIC ROMANCES THROUGH THE AGES

1. Samson and Delilah
2. Narcissus and himself
3. Paris and Helen of Troy
4. Henry VIII and any one of his six wives
5. Barbie and Ken

My days of missing it—or him—are long past me now, and they are about to be long past for you too. Now I am ruined. Completely ruined. Spoiled for mundane life. Incapable of tolerating love that is built on looks, popularity, and what-can-you-do-for-me behavior. Revolutionary love got me. *His* revolutionary love.

His love is extreme—breaking free from all that is traditional and accepted in this world. Immoderate—the opposite of the plastic, fake, hyperemotional whirlwind that this planet claims to be real. He has built a true foundation—a place from which authentic love can grow in every capacity this life offers. The result—a passion so deep, it has become the basis for the person I am.

This is what has revolutionized my life. He has completely torn down and replaced everything I had been pressured to believe was love. He brought change that began in an instant, yet evolved over time into a relationship for eternity.

Nothing is like it because no one is like him.

If you want this—a radical passion that revolutionizes your life—read on. You'll find it here. If not, you might just want to re-gift this book. For those who are committed to continue, you are about to find what and who you have always looked for—even if you didn't know you were looking.

Feelings of wanting to be wanted ruled my life for a long time. Recently, Brittany confided to me while crying, *"I'm the only one of all of my friends who hasn't had a boyfriend! The kids in lunch today were making fun of me because I've never been kissed!"*

Brittany felt that pain because her definition of being wanted was the same as theirs. We've all been there one time or another, believing things that were not true. *I'm not beautiful. I'm not as valuable as other girls.*

Do you struggle day to day with similar pain? Tough stuff like waiting for the right guy, not doing what it seems everyone else is doing, and keeping a clean heart and mind? I struggled with all that too, and still do sometimes.

GUY
+
ME
=
VALUE
???

Eight years old. That's the earliest memory I have of Jesus' pursuit of me. My mom shared with me her new relationship with Christ; I wanted what she had. So I knelt by our coffee table and asked him to forgive me for my sins and be my life. After that, my heart really wanted to do right, but the older I became, the harder that was! Making right choices often meant doing the opposite of what many of my friends were doing.

As I went through school, my convictions grew stronger and stronger, but my heart still felt weak. Doing all the right stuff didn't take away the loneliness. Lying in my bed in the dark, listening to love songs, only made my sadness stronger. Making wise choices made me glad; being on the "outside" didn't.

Rachel, a sophomore, felt the same way: *"Doing the right thing all of the time and being different gets tiring."*

I can relate. During all that time in high school, I didn't realize that *he* wanted me and could fill the cavern in my heart. Bible school (a nine-month training program) came next. Dropping me off at my dorm a thousand miles away from home, my parents were back on the road again after just a twenty-minute stay. You want to talk about being lonely?

But surrounded by no one I knew, I was exactly where I needed to be. In the middle of this lonely place, I found true love. It happened when my school counselor passed on this message to me—a note from a "friend":

I think you are so beautiful, Lynn. . . . Let me start at your feet and go all the way to your head. Your toes are so pretty . . . they each should have a ring on them and then be slipped into soft and lovely slippers fit for a princess. Your hands are so soft, with fingers that are slender and feminine . . . a diamond placed on each one. Your arms are strong and defined, but perfect for a lady . . . they each deserve silk gloves to your delicate elbows. Your cheeks are smooth and rosy, surrounding a smile that is captivating. Just looking at your hair makes me want to run my fingers through it and never stop!

Stunned, I thought, *Really? Is this true? Someone out there really sees me this way?* I was a little leery. In high school, one of the stars of the football team sent me a flower for one of those fund-raisers at school with a note that said, "I want to ask you out." I felt ecstatic . . . until the yucky feelings swept in. He was a popular senior. I was a sophomore nobody. *Had I been the brunt of a joke?* Quickly shoving the white carnation into my bag, I tried to shove down all the swirling hurt in my heart.

Memories like that made me afraid that this love might also be empty. But my counselor kept passing on the notes:

Dear Friend and Love, You're beautiful! Don't look at me! When you look at me, I can't think straight. Your beauty is too much for me—I'm in over my head. I'm not used to this! I can't take it in. Your hair flows and shimmers . . . there is no one like you on earth, never has been, never will be. You are like no one I have ever met. You are perfect. Everyone who knows you admires you . . . before I knew what was happening, my heart was raptured, carried away by thoughts of only you!

Have you ever heard of falling for someone you have never even seen? These words created the perfect picture of what I wanted—what I'd been looking for all along. Note number three sealed it:

How beautiful you are! Oh, how beautiful!

Short and sweet.

Read the messages again. Listen to them. How emotional! Hands sweaty, stomach full of butterflies, heart pounding.

When I heard that all of these notes were words from the Bible, from a book called the Song of Solomon (adapted from Song of Solomon 6, 7:1-6, and 6:9, *The Message*), I was shocked. I had never known that God could have these feelings—that Jesus could feel *this* way about me. I had grown up knowing him as my savior, leader, and best friend, but no one had ever spoken of this type of love! Some of my friends had boyfriends who told them, "I love you." But come on. How powerful can love really be after two weeks?

Like a girl with her first boyfriend, I read my "love notes" over and over and over again. Exploring these treasure-filled verses changed everything for me. Two changes in particular started to happen right away. Verses like these seemed to show up often whenever I read the Bible. (They had always been there, but since I hadn't known God felt such strong love for me, I had just never really seen them!) I also began to feel differently. As I filled my mind and heart with these words of love from Jesus, my loneliness left me—there was no room for it! I began to see myself differently. The desperate need to be perfect inside and out began to fade.

> **SOLOMON WAS QUITE THE ROMANTIC.**
>
> Then again, he had lots of practice—the king of Israel (970–930 BC) had 700 wives and 300 concubines! If you wonder what God thought about that, check out the story in 1 Kings 11.

I'm sure that you feel so much pressure to be perfect inside and out too, especially if you want to get the attention of guys. Eighteen-year-old Zach told me, *"I wish girls didn't feel like they have to look perfect."* Easy for him to say, right? He doesn't have to deal with the TV starlets with their ultra-smooth skin, the magazine models with their airbrushed bodies, or the mall mannequins with their size 2 silhouettes!

As I let the true words of Jesus melt into my heart, my own fears that I would never find the "right guy" began to melt away. There was already one who said I was his! From that time until now, this powerful relationship with Jesus has grown stronger and stronger.

That gives you a glimpse of how I fell for this revolutionary love. *His* revolutionary love. Like I did, you probably still think this sounds a bit strange. Don't freak out—just keep reading.

I really hope that you are getting the opportunity to go through this book with some of your best friends and a woman who also loves Jesus. If not, text a friend now and see if she'd join you. A friend makes everything better, right?

A glance at the Contents page will tell you the book is divided into three parts: 1) In "His Heart Toward Me," we'll talk about how and what God is communicating to you; 2) In "His Path for Me," we'll think about what our behavior needs to be to show we love God; and 3) In "His Hopes for Me," we'll dream together about what amazing, crazy, radical things we can do with the knowledge of his revolutionary love.

Along the way, you'll get to hear from other girls who have hung out with me—some your age, some older—girls who understand and have been where you are. And you'll get a chance to put down your own thoughts where questions and space have been provided for you to do a little journaling. I've included some of my own diary entries too. (Sorry, I left out all the really juicy bits!) At the end of each chapter, you'll find Connection, which gives you a chance to talk to Jesus, and Radical Pursuits, a section designed to make you think about how specifically Jesus is pursuing you, and how you can respond. Peppered throughout the book, you'll find lots of wisdom from the best source of all, God's Word.

So grab your Bible. Let's start at the beginning of this love story—one that isn't going to break your heart.

CHAPTER ~ 1

He Wants Me

"The king is wild for you."

—Psalm 45:11 (*The Message*)

*L*ike most girls, Jo experienced loneliness and emptiness. I met her when she was in ninth grade. She followed Jesus, but had never seen the side of him that truly loved her. Jo recently shared with me:

> In high school, I often felt fat or would hear lies in my head like 'I'm not good, skinny, or pretty enough to have a boyfriend.' Or 'You don't have any friends because no one likes you.'

Have you ever felt this way? Unliked. Unwanted. Exactly the opposite of what you *want* to feel? I know I have.

I want to feel cherished, loved, and valued. You can even see it in my movie choices.

I sit in the dark room, my heart beating wildly. "Hurry! Hurry!" my brain cries out. "You'll be too late!" You'd think I'd never seen *Pirates of the Caribbean*. But I have. A bunch of times. I know that Will Turner *will* get there just in time. I know he will swing to Elizabeth's rescue right at the last second, yell "She goes free!" to the captain and his crew, and risk his life to save hers. It doesn't matter that I already know all of that. The thrill of the pursuit sends my heart pounding every time.

Why? Maybe there's something wrong with me. But I know I'm not alone. Lots of girls love to watch the same chick flicks over and

ROMANCES WORTH WATCHING AGAIN

1. *Pirates of the Caribbean*
2. *Sense and Sensibility*
3. *50 First Dates*
4. *The Princess Bride*
5. *A Walk to Remember*

over again, especially the ones where the hero gives everything to get the girl. Like the girl in the movie, we want to be desired, fought for, pursued—wanted.

Who is this coming from Edom,
from Bozrah, with his garments stained crimson?
Who is this, robed in splendor,
striding forward in the greatness of his strength?
"It is I, speaking in righteousness, mighty to save."
—Isaiah 63:1

CRAZY GIRL

As soon as I discovered boys, my heart wanted someone to be crazy for me. Someone to notice me. I can still remember my first phone call from Greg. I ran up the stairs, slamming the door to my room so no one would hear our conversation. I wanted to shout, "Somebody really likes me!" (I didn't. My parents would have said, "Tell him to quit calling!")

Someone was pursuing me. Someone wanted to spend time with *me*. I see this same desire in girls over and over again. We get so excited when a guy makes a nice comment about our Facebook picture or compliments us at school. We're human. We crave love, affection, attention.

Greg eventually quit calling, but I still wanted his attention (even though I didn't get it). For *years*. I'm not exaggerating— seven to be exact! I liked him, but he always gave his attention to someone else.

Sometimes we'll go to crazy lengths to get that love, affection, and attention that we want *so* bad. I used to walk by our high school's football field during practice, just looking for Greg's number. I would drive by the gym, hoping to catch a glimpse of him as he got off work. I'd bike past his house, thinking he might possibly be out mowing the lawn. (Don't think I'm weird. You do it too—it's called Facebook stalking!) Sometimes I would write my first name with his last name over and over and over again, covering my notebook.

If I couldn't have what I wanted, I would pretend in my heart that I did.

This make-believe behavior of mine went on for a really long time. Until a good friend of mine helped me discover a love I didn't have to make up. She introduced me to unconditional, unfailing love that blew me away. Love, affection, and attention—everything I wanted. It wasn't what I expected—didn't come from *where* I expected.

And we, out of all creation, became his prized possession.
—James 1:18 (*NLT*)

So where did it come from? Words. But not just any words. The Word. Multitudes of love notes to me, just waiting to be read, loaded with the truth—I'm valued. To make me understand that these words were for me, my friend taught me to put my name in the verses. Go ahead, put your name in here too.

Dear (insert your name here),
Don't miss a word: forget your
country, put your home behind you.

> Be here—the king is wild for you. Since he's your lord, adore him."
> (Psalm 45:10, 11, The Message)

Someone was pursuing me, but not in the way I expected—not like what happens in the movies, at school, or at prom. Jesus wanted me. And when I didn't respond right away, he came for me again.

> Don't be afraid. . . . I've called your name. You're mine. . . . I paid a huge price for you. . . . That's how much you mean to me! That's how much I love you! I'd sell off the whole world to get you back, trade the creation just for you."
> (Isaiah 43:1, 4, The Message)

He says he loves us enough to sell off the whole world to get us back. Give up everything on the planet just for me? That's crazy! But that's the radical love that revolutionizes lives.

Have you ever thought of Jesus caring for you like that? Why or why not? Use this space for journaling your thoughts.

When I learned these verses, I began to see a side of Jesus I had never seen before. He wanted to be more than the God I served. He wanted to be the God I loved. He wanted me to know him, but not just as a rule maker. He wanted to be the love of my life. My *everything*.

I had a really hard time getting it, really understanding him. I mean, when I read the Bible then, I read rules. Have you ever thought that? It's just a book of rules? So when I started reading these words of love, I had to ask myself, "What's wrong with my thinking? Why am I so messed up that it's hard for me to accept this perfect, unconditional love?" I knew that my own insecurities had something to do with it. A boyfriend, an incredible grade point average, school records in sports. I had none of those. I messed up sometimes, did things that caused others to be disappointed in me. So why would he love *me* like that?

 JEALOUS JESUS

God wired us for love—to give and receive. We might naturally look to guys to fill our hearts, but that type of love is not complete (though it can sometimes feel like it!). Guys just don't have what it takes to fill the empty space inside us. Jesus does. When we soak in his words, enough to have it really in our hearts, we believe. We believe the truth that we are special and beautiful. If we never discover the depth of this incredible love, that special spot in our heart remains empty.

You see, Jesus is jealous. Is that a radical thought to you? Jesus—jealous? Yes, he is jealous for you. He created you to experience the closest love possible between the two of you. He doesn't want us to fill our hearts with anyone or anything other than himself!

> And do you suppose God doesn't care? The proverb has it that "he's a fiercely jealous lover." And what he gives in love is far better than anything else you'll find.
> —James 4:5 (*The Message*)

Sometimes, we can be stubborn. We try filling our hearts with friends, guys, accomplishments, sex, drugs, sports. But these things—or anything—cannot fill this space created solely for him. We may be temporarily happy or enjoy a good time, but in the end we will always come up short.

Hannah, age fifteen, put it this way:

I had always looked to my friends, boyfriend, and family for happiness, but they can only bring so much. I had to learn God was the only one that could truly bring me complete fulfillment. Don't ever expect to be happy if you're looking at the world for happiness. You won't find it.

For some of us, the absence of a father—or the lack of his love—can make the hole in our hearts even bigger. As a very quiet man, my dad had a hard time showing love. I knew he loved me, but he wasn't home much, nor was he affectionate. Every day I saw him work so hard to provide for my family; I know those actions proved his love for me, but I longed to *hear* it. Yet he never said those four little words: "I love you, Lynn." It wasn't until I was no longer the little girl who wanted to crawl up in his lap that I heard him say those words.

Just when I finally felt his love and he voiced the words that I had always longed to hear—"I'm proud of you" and "I love you too"—just then, he died. This left a huge hole in my heart. But my father, even if he had been the perfect dad, would never have been able to fill me up. God didn't create him to fill that role. Love from a guy, be it a dad or a boyfriend, can never fill the love gap in our hearts. Only Jesus can.

How do you think your relationship (or lack of relationship) with your dad has affected the way you receive God's love?

HE'S SPEAKING MY LANGUAGE

Have you ever thought God was trying to get your attention? Lately, I've begun discovering what I call surprises from him. Jesus attempts to speak his love to me—even when I am not looking for it. Some days, it's something gorgeous he made, like an incredible sunset that blows me away. Other days, I recognize the gifts of relationships, just like Mariah saw on her fifteenth birthday—not through presents, but in text after text that came, wishing her a great day. I also see his love in the way he takes care of me and provides for what I need. Recently, I had an incredible day—whitewater rafting in the morning, a long walk with my dog in the afternoon, and a game of disc golf after supper with my family. At the end of the day, I wore a huge smile and knew my day had been a gift from God.

He's trying to get your attention too: a new friendship, days where everything seems to go just right, or someone shows that they love you just the way you are. But even on the bad days (when nothing goes right—your parents fight, your dog runs away, your best friend ignores you, and you fail your math quiz), God is still with you and he still loves you!

"*I'm still searching for my and God's love language. . . . I can't wait to find it.*" Fourteen-year-old Jessica is listening for the way God is speaking to her. Reflect for a moment on your own life. Could he be trying to get your attention?

Sometimes I think that some of God's love messages to us are hidden. Proverbs 25:2 says "It is the glory of God to conceal a matter." He likes being a little mysterious! Have you ever hidden something, secretly hoping it would be found? Recently while traveling alone, I unpacked my bag and discovered a card popping out from under a pile of clothes. "You're going to do great!" was on a handwritten note. How cool! Someone who loves me had hidden this special note of encouragement.

That's exactly what the Bible is: one HUGE note, filled with stories and examples of God's revolutionary love for you.

Take a few moments and write out how you think Jesus would describe you.

Grab your Bible because I want you to look up the verses that I'm going to give you. When you find them, underline them or write them down on something you keep with you. Someday you might be feeling very lonely or even unloved. At that time, when you most need to feel God's loving arms, reread these words!

First look up Song of Solomon 4:7: "All beautiful you are, my darling; there is no flaw in you."

No flaw! In another version, these words are interpreted as "no blemish." The study notes in my Bible explain this as *hyperbole*—exaggerated speech used to emphasize something the writer is trying to communicate *(New International Version Hebrew-Greek Key Word Study Bible* [Chattanooga, Tennessee: AMG Publishers, 1996], 790). You may see zits, dull hair, and an imperfect nose, but Jesus sees something entirely different.

Not only does he see you as perfect, but what does Song of Solomon 7:10 say that God wants—more than anything? "I am my lover's. I'm all he wants. I'm all the world to him!" (*The Message*).

You! *You!* God wants you!

Lots of us grow up thinking that the Christian life is about doing. What about you? Have you ever believed in this formula: Good Deeds + More Good Deeds = God's Approval? That's one equation that will never add up. What Jesus wants is a relationship—an intimate relationship—with you! He died for it.

Maybe you already know your actions alone don't make you a Christian—faith does. Let's see what your faith can do.

 ## LOVE TATTOO

Tattoos are big these days, especially "love" ones. You know the kind—the name of someone's sweetheart inked in big bold letters. Well, you know what? They're nothing new. Thousands of years ago, the Bible talked about a tattoo of sorts: "Place me like a seal over your heart, like a seal on your arm" (Song of Solomon 8:6).

Jesus has your name inscribed on his body—and this is no

cheap, rub-on tattoo. He's not the type who is here today and gone tomorrow. He's not the type who says you mean everything to him tonight, and then doesn't call you again. He *is* love: permanent, powerful, and persistent.

Love is invincible facing danger and death.
Passion laughs at the terrors of hell.
The fire of love stops at nothing—
it sweeps everything before it.
Flood waters can't drown love,
torrents of rain can't put it out.
Love can't be bought, love can't be sold—
it's not to be found in the marketplace.
—Song of Solomon 8:6-8 (*The Message*)

Because his love is permanent, powerful, and persistent, you can depend on him. You can trust him with the hard things, with your deepest secrets. And you can rest in the security that no matter what happens or what you do, his strong love sticks by you through it all. He will always be there! You can count on him!

 **Connection**

Make a connection with the one who wants you more than anything. Pray:

Jesus, this is all really new to me. To think that you love me this much—it's all just a bit

overwhelming and even feels weird. Help me to grasp this truth and begin to love you the way you love me! Amen.

Radical Pursuits

Remember the first girl in this chapter—Jo? Have you ever felt bad about yourself like she did? Where did these feelings come from? Were they mostly from you, or from something someone did, said, or didn't do?

> **Think about an event or a time when you were feeling negative about yourself. Write out what happened.**

Now read how Jo finally got just how much Jesus loved her:

After high school I did a discipleship

training school with Youth with a Mission where I went through three phases: learning about God, sharing what I learned about God, and applying and extending what I learned about God; like being on a honeymoon with Jesus. He really did have me all to himself, and I wanted to have that time with only him. Usually people don't have the opportunity to take an extended amount of time to really just BE with Jesus, which is what he wants most! He wants to show us that love.

"On a honeymoon with Jesus." OK, so you're busy. You've got stuff. But right now, do something radical. Take the time to realize Jesus is pursuing you.

Rewrite your story—the one that put you in a negative mood. Only this time, have Jesus come to your rescue. Using some of the verses we have looked up, have him repeat these words to you.

The next time that voice of negativity whispers in your brain, play these words of Jesus back in your mind, letting his words of love, attention, and affection comfort you. Remember that he wants you!

CHAPTER ~ 2

He Knows Me

"He will take great delight in you;
in his love he will no longer rebuke you,
but will rejoice over you with singing."

—Zephaniah 3:17

I had it going on (or at least I thought I did!): part of the youth leadership at church, a good student, running on the cross country team, selected for elite music groups at school—singing solos in church was even common for me. Not getting in trouble or hanging out with those who did—it was all part of my plan. Being good was what others wanted, what they expected of me.

I wonder now, was that the real me? What about those parts of me that weren't so good? Did anyone know the real me? If they had known, would they have loved me?

Can any of you relate? Maybe on the outside you too appear to have it all together, but things aren't so together on the inside. Do you ever feel like you're faking it? Do you find yourself every day performing a certain way, trying to keep up with the expectations of parents, teachers, coaches, and friends? Maybe you feel no one really gets you.

For me, the inside was not as good as the outside. Every few weeks, I would reevaluate my life, especially my thought life. I would tell Jesus he could have complete control of my life . . . again. My sense of being a failure seemed to swallow me up. Surely when Jesus looked at me, he was disappointed in me.

 ALL OF ME

Truth be told, he wasn't disappointed in me. In fact, although he knew everything—the stuff others saw and the stuff they didn't—he still loved me.

The same is true with you. He knows it all and he loves you. Even when we make bad decisions, shameful decisions (things we would be mortified for our parents to discover), he knows, and it doesn't change the way he feels about us. It doesn't alter or erase his love! Maria, age fourteen, told me, "*One of the lies I struggle with is I am who I am based on what I do. Drawing closer to him has helped me to realize that it is OK if I am not good at everything!*"

So here's what I want you to do. If there's a Bible nearby, grab it. (If not, keep reading down a few lines in this book and you'll find a chunk of Bible verses.) Turn to the middle. You'll probably land in a book called Psalms. It has a lot of chapters, or psalms. Locate Psalm 139. It will be broken down into smaller parts. I want you to read the first eighteen parts (verses). Read these verses out loud, listening to Jesus speak to you. Yes, out loud. You might feel weird, but go ahead. You need to *hear* this truth as you read it.

You have searched me, Lord,
and you know me.
You know when I sit and when I rise;
you perceive my thoughts from afar.
You discern my going out and my lying down;
you are familiar with all my ways.
Before a word is on my tongue
you, Lord, know it completely.
You hem me in behind and before,
and you lay your hand upon me.
Such knowledge is too wonderful for me,
too lofty for me to attain.

THE BOOK OF PSALMS is a collection of ancient prayers, poems, and songs, many of which were written by David, a king of Israel. The psalms cover a wide range of human emotions and experiences, as well as descriptions of the characteristics, actions, and promises of God.

He Knows Me

Where can I go from your Spirit?
Where can I flee from your presence?
If I go up to the heavens, you are there;
if I make my bed in the depths, you are there.
If I rise on the wings of the dawn,
if I settle on the far side of the sea,
even there your hand will guide me,
your right hand will hold me fast.
If I say, "Surely the darkness will hide me
and the light become night around me,"
even the darkness will not be dark to you;
the night will shine like the day,
for darkness is as light to you.
For you created my inmost being;
you knit me together in my mother's womb.
I praise you because I am fearfully and wonderfully made;
your works are wonderful,
I know that full well.
My frame was not hidden from you
when I was made in the secret place,
when I was woven together in the depths of the earth.
Your eyes saw my unformed body;
all the days ordained for me were written in your book
before one of them came to be.
How precious to me are your thoughts, God!
How vast is the sum of them!
Were I to count them,
they would outnumber the grains of sand—
when I awake, I am still with you.

—Psalm 139:1-18

Did you hear that Jesus loves *every* part of you? (If you skipped it or sped through it, go back. You've got to read this—it's completely worth it!) Ever hear the saying "love is blind"? Well this love isn't! Jesus knows you. He knows everything you do, everything you've done, and everything you even *think* about doing. Does any of it change the way he feels about you? No! Where can you go and be too far away from his love? Nowhere!

How do you feel about the fact that he knows everything about you and still loves you?

Even knowing our deepest thoughts, our darkest deeds, and our disappointing attitudes doesn't change his loving thoughts toward us. Here's what used to hang me up: I knew that he loved me unconditionally, but I thought he would *like* me more, *approve* of me more when I did everything right. Of course, it brings joy to his heart when we obey. He wants us to obey because it points others to him and he knows that the best things in life come through obedience to God. But, our actions and who we are do not affect his love for us. Our actions do not make him love us more; they do not make him love us less.

So go ahead, be completely honest with him. Why not? He already knows the things we hang on to tightly in our hearts—our fears, dreams, hurts, and hopes. Your parents might be shocked or surprised by things in your life, but he isn't! He may not be pleased with everything we do, but his love never, ever wavers. He deeply cares about all aspects of what makes up the person called you.

What is one area of your life that you have a hard time conceiving Jesus knows about and still loves you so much?

Sometimes, though, even with learning just how crazy he is about us, we can still feel low. Listen as God describes the action he took to show you his plan of love (Hosea 11:4, *NKJV*):

> *I drew them with gentle cords,*
> *With bands of love,*
> *And I was to them as those who*
> *   take the yoke from their neck.*
> *I stooped and fed them.*

He stooped in order to love us in a way we could understand and receive. He bent down to meet us where we were so we could get the depth of his love. He doesn't ask us to change to become lovable. He comes to us, exactly as we are, and helps us to love him right back.

His stooping to draw us closer to him may mean reminding us of the truth, like it did for Emily, a recent Clemson graduate:

> *There was a time in college when I was doing something that I knew I shouldn't be. I would hear in my mind and heart all of the verses that I had learned when I was in middle*

WE PLEASE HIM MOST, NOT BY FRANTICALLY TRYING TO MAKE OURSELVES GOOD, BUT BY THROWING OURSELVES INTO HIS ARMS WITH ALL OUR IMPERFECTIONS, AND BELIEVING THAT HE UNDERSTANDS EVERYTHING AND LOVES US STILL!

—A.W. Tozer,
The Root of the Righteous

He Knows Me

school and high school. It was like they were
saying to me "Remember who you are!" Knowing
the truth helped me to get my life back on
track with him.

Verses like the ones in Psalms helped Emily return to a growing relationship with Jesus. Re-read Psalm 139:13-16 in *The Message:*

> *Oh yes, you shaped me first inside, then out;*
> *you formed me in my mother's womb.*
> *I thank you, High God—you're breathtaking!*
> *Body and soul, I am marvelously made!*
> *I worship in adoration—what a creation!*
> *You know me inside and out,*
> *you know every bone in my body;*
> *You know exactly how I was made, bit by bit,*
> *how I was sculpted from nothing into something.*
> *Like an open book, you watched me grow from*
>   *conception to birth;*
> *all the stages of my life were spread out before you.*

BEAUTIFUL OUTSIDE

Christians may talk a lot about beauty on the inside, but that isn't the only beauty that God sees. He sees us as beautiful on the outside too! Psalm 45 is another place in the Bible that gives us a picture of Jesus Christ and his followers as being like a marriage. In this song it is a marriage between a king and his queen. In Psalm 45:11 the picture is of the king being "enthralled by your beauty." Jesus is enthralled by the beauty of you!

God is a creator: the one who makes things beautiful. As the perfect artisan, his perfect workmanship is in you! Your eyes, your hair, your shape, your personality—he knows each part of you, and sees you as beautiful, because you are his creation.

Jesus also knows that it is important to us to feel beautiful. That's another reason for us to take in the truth of how he sees us. Our hearts and minds long for someone to look at us and believe that we are gorgeous. Our creator does!

Even when we realize this truth, sometimes we might think that something about us could have been made better. Does he? Remember Song of Solomon 4:7 from the last chapter?

Look up the verse and write it down below.

God doesn't say "I see no blemish in you." He says "there *is* no blemish in you." Written specifically for you, this verse goes against the ways that we often see ourselves. He knows we look for the worst in ourselves and put ourselves down some days. He knows that when we look in the mirror and in our hearts, we don't see what he sees. He knows we need to hear truth in order to experience acceptance and joy.

 ## IN THE BEHOLDER'S EYE

Song of Solomon 5:2 (*NKJV*) says it another way: "Open for me, my sister, my love, My dove, my perfect one." You might be tempted to say "How can he say 'my perfect one'? Get real!" He says "perfect one" because when he sees you, when you have accepted Jesus as your Savior, he doesn't see your sin—he sees his forgiveness. His

He's not mad at you, he's mad about you.

—Rick Warren,
The Purpose Driven Life

forgiveness makes us pure, removing our sins or transgressions: "For as high as the heavens are above the earth, so great is his love for those who fear him; as far as the east is from the west, so far has he removed our transgressions from us" (Psalm 103:11, 12).

The word *transgressions* in that verse refers to actions that offend God's character and act against his will. For example, say you want to go to a movie. You ask your parents and they say no, but you go anyway. The Bible says to obey our parents, so when we don't, it's sin; we not only offend our parents, we offend God. We may suffer consequences for our actions, such as punishment from our parents or damaging the trust our parents have in us. But when we ask for forgiveness from God, we are saved from his punishment and receive his mercy instead. He wipes our record clean; it is as if those offenses never occurred.

So how come Jesus can do that—just wipe those sins away as if they never happened? Jesus, who is perfect, *chose* to leave Heaven and come to imperfect earth to live among us and die for us. Justice required payment for our sin, a way to make us right before God. Only the perfect one could do that.

Do you like to buy music or other things online? When you do, you have to pay for it. So, maybe you ask your parents to borrow their credit card because you don't have one. In order to get what you want, someone has to pay for it!

We could never pay the price to get the forgiveness we need. Being good couldn't do it. Only one perfect person could—Jesus. Compelled by love, he paid the costly price of a horrible, painful death on a wretched chunk of wood. His death payment covers our imperfections and things we have done against him. Those of us who receive the benefit of this payment by asking for it have been made new. Flaw free. Now when he looks at us, he sees no blemishes because of what he has done—and in spite of what *we* have done!

That is what makes this radical love so revolutionary, completely different from other love. He loves, knowing who he created us to be. Who do you know who loves like that? I never had a boyfriend who loved me like that. Even our family struggles to love us at such a selfless level! Perfect love—that is what makes this love so drastically different.

HE LOVES, IN SPITE OF OUR WORST PARTS.

He Knows Me

Have you ever had a friend or boyfriend find out something about you that seemed to change the way they saw you or felt about you? How did that scenario make you feel?

YOU'VE GOT GOD'S HEART

Listen to Song of Solomon 4:9 (*NKJV*): "You have ravished my heart With one *look* of your eyes, With one link of your necklace." I just love that! *Ravished* sounds like a cool word, but what does it mean?

Webster's Universal College Dictionary says *ravish* means:

1) *to transport with strong emotion especially joy*

2) *to seize and carry off by force*

3) *to rob*

4) *to captivate*

5) *to enchant*

Sounds like the movie I watched last night. Have you seen *Ever After*? Henry just can't get Danielle out of his mind! Though she is a commoner and he is the crown prince, the difference can't break the spell. She has ravished his heart.

The first time I read Song of Solomon 4:9 telling me I had ravished the heart of the King of the universe, I found myself smiling from ear to ear and even heard myself giggle! Some versions of the Bible translate 4:9 differently. One says "You have stolen my heart" (*NIV*). You have stolen the heart of the King of Heaven! He can't get over you!

You may be saying "If he feels that way about everyone, how does that make me special?" Have you ever created something with your own hands? It doesn't matter how many times you do it, there's still something special about a thing you have made all on your own. You have a special connection to that thing because *you* made it. God *created* you. Only one you. No one like you. Unique, individual, rare, uncommon, exceptional, valuable, significant YOU!

PASSION COMPELS HIM

This passionate love compels Jesus to pursue you, to not settle until the two of you have the closest relationship possible! He wants you to come to him with all of your life stuff—excitement, hurts, joys, and pains. Just as he knows you, he wants you to know him too! He wants to share his heart with you—his excitement, hurts, joys, and pains.

I hope this truth is beginning to sink into your heart. It may take a while; be patient. It's not every day that you find out that the God of the universe is stuck on you!

He Knows Me

Connection

Make a connection with the one who wants you more than anything. Pray:

> *Thank you, God, for this tremendous love you have for me. Work the truth of your love deep in my heart— that you know everything about me and still love me. Your love never changes. Cause my love for you to grow. I know you will do it because you want to! Amen.*

Radical Pursuits

Grab a sheet of paper or use the space provided. At the top write "Dear Jesus." (Don't say you'll do this later. Do it now! I know you're tempted to say that, because I sometimes do when I am reading an interactive book!) Write a love note to Jesus. Start out by giving him thanks for perfectly loving you, no matter what. Remember that part about yourself that you wish he didn't know? Ask him to forgive you for going against his ways and offending him. After that, thank him for forgiveness and for seeing the best in you. Finish by asking him to help you open your life every day to him and return this radical love.

Write your love note to Jesus here.

CHAPTER ~ 3

He Speaks to Me

"My heart has heard you say,
'Come and talk with me.'
And my heart responds, 'Lord, I am coming.'"

—Psalm 27:8 (*NLT*)

*D*ifferent. In a good way. For five days Katie had been at camp; away from TV, cell phones, Facebook. She really felt like she had met Jesus there. Finding out just how crazy he was about her made her heart soar. Hearing from him wasn't hard at camp. Incredible worship music made her feel close to him. Dynamic speakers caused her to sense his presence. Her schedule made reading the Bible and praying easy; no distractions were around. It seemed Jesus and she were on one long date together.

But now at home . . . well, things were just different.

Have you ever had what some might call a mountaintop experience? Feeling like you couldn't get any closer to God? Your only hope is the feeling will stay, but you doubt it will.

Roller-coaster experiences make our relationship with Jesus seem unstable, unpredictable—like your first crush, which only lasted five days. On campfire nights emotions and convictions burn hot, but then we have to return to the "real" world. Can Jesus whisper to us every day in the middle of biology, softball tournaments, and jobs?

Yes he can and wants to! Even though your environment has changed, he hasn't. Isaiah 54:10 says "Though the mountains be shaken and the hills be removed, yet my unfailing love for you will not be shaken." His love impels him to speak to you.

No matter what is going on, good or bad, Jesus' desire to speak to us never changes. So if he never changes, what does? Us.

Two people who have a crush want to be together all the time, right? A girl and a guy who just met yesterday suddenly seem inseparable today. Now, everything they do, they do together. The same is true when we are in love with Jesus, when his love has completely changed our world. We will want to spend time with him. That's how we learn to hear him speak—spending time with him.

IF HE NEVER CHANGES, WHAT DOES?

Consider what made your mountaintop experience special. The music? Find amazing worship music on the Internet and put it on your iPod. The speaker? The Internet gives you access to excellent, godly speakers 24/7. Reading the Bible and prayer? Do it at home. You see, it is all available to you. The difference is that your schedule was set *for* you at camp. The difference was there were fewer distractions at camp. When we return home, *we* become the schedule makers; we have to make time to hear from him ourselves. Hopefully—just like the guy and girl who are crazy about each other—spending time with him is something you want to do!

FEELINGS DON'T EQUAL LOVE

You just saw him. Your heart starts pounding; you feel giddy inside. You've got a crush. Sometimes, we have the same kinds of feelings about God. We equate emotional experiences with hearing from him, but feelings can't always be duplicated. That doesn't make emotional experiences about God bad. What you experienced at camp was real; it wasn't fake. Feelings are just not dependable. They aren't enough to build a relationship. Feelings don't have depth; they change all the time. We can't count on our emotions to tell us when God is speaking to us.

I woke up on a Saturday morning and just lay in bed. You know when you are awake, but you don't really want to be? (I bet you've even pretended to be asleep some mornings, because you knew that when you got up, a to-do list would be waiting! I know I've done that!) As soon as my eyes popped open, my mind started whirling with negative thoughts: "You really aren't a good friend"; "You're not as strong a Christian as you think you are"; along with plenty of other depressing ideas. I didn't feel like a Christian; I didn't sense that Jesus was near. I did have a sense I better do something or my whole day was going to head in the wrong direction. Putting on my running shoes, I headed out the front door for a long run . . . with Jesus.

As I ran, I cried. I told him how I was feeling. That's when I began to remember all the Bible verses I had memorized.

It didn't matter how I felt. How I felt didn't change how he felt about me or the fact that I was his. Having read his Word, I knew his Word; truth came to me as I ran down the street. He spoke to me as his Word came back to my mind.

GREAT WAYS TO START YOUR DAY

1. Read your Bible.
2. Pray.
3. Go for a walk, run, skip, swim, or ride. Listen for what God has to say to you along the way.
4. Three words: chocolate chip oatmeal. (OK, maybe that's just a great start to *my* day!)

When do you find you most want to hear from Jesus? When you are happy and you want someone to share it? When you are sad or mad? Write about it here.

Elizabeth, age sixteen, said this,

> When it comes to how I feel about Jesus, I would have to say different. I don't feel the things that others describe, and yet I know he is always with me. It's more intellectual, I guess, than emotional.

I like what Elizabeth said. Since feelings aren't reliable, we need to seek to hear him speak to us no matter how we feel. But how? Seeking to hear him begins with his love letter, the Bible. Jeremiah 29:13 says, "You will seek me and find me when you seek me with all your heart."

When we do seek him—reading the Bible with the expectation that we'll hear—we can find new truths every time we read. It never gets old!

Mary, age fourteen, described how she hears from God:

> When I'm reading my Bible, I think of God and I reminiscing together, especially when I'm reading a story. I settle in and he tells me about things he's done. We're very comfortable—God and I.

I do need to warn you: reading the Bible can be dangerous. Really, I'm not just being cheesy. Reading truth changes you. Maybe you are like Emma, who described her relationship with Jesus as usual, routine, normal, but what she wants it to be is spontaneous and dynamic. Reading the Bible can be! Jesus is countercultural—

different from the crowd. Grasping his truth transforms your heart and mind. How cool is that? Romans 12:2 calls this "renewing" our minds.

It's like changing up the library on your iPod. The more consistent you are about reading the Bible, the more you will replace the old tracks your brain plays with the new tracks of what the Bible says is true. Truths like these: "I am loved!" and "I was created to be his!" This is one way that he speaks to us: when his words come back to our thoughts after we have read them or meditated on them. Katie shared with me that when she finds verses that really stick out to her, she writes them on her mirror with dry-erase markers so she can read them every morning.

His Revolutionary Love

 # AWAY FROM THE NOISE

Reminders of Jesus' words, like the marker messages on Katie's mirror, help us during the day—especially when the noise of everything around us gets louder and louder. Noise usually isn't a problem when you're chatting or texting your best friend, but sometimes with Jesus it's different (especially if you aren't used to having a relationship with him). It takes time and effort to learn to hear him.

A very important part of learning to hear God speak is silence. In the Bible there are several passages that talk about Jesus getting alone and being quiet in order to hear God speak. Check these out: "After leaving them, he went up on a mountainside to pray" (Mark 6:46); "Jesus often withdrew to lonely places and prayed" (Luke 5:16).

> **MY DIARY**
> Entry from April (age eighteen): "I got up at 5:30 today to spend time with Jesus out in the field behind school. Nothing extraordinary happened, but I was there and it was good."

Silence is unheard of in our world. Constantly surrounded by noise, we like the music of busyness. Some of that noise isn't even sounds we hear, but messages in our brains. We want our cells available 24/7—gotta be able to read every text! Checking out the latest posts, tweets, status updates, and celebrity headlines is vital. A GPS calling out directions as we head somewhere new is comforting. Add TV, iPods, and radios and you have constant, consistent noise. How can we hear God speak when everything around us is so loud?

Look again at Jesus. He got away and got quiet to hear from God. He spent significant amounts of time alone with his Father.

When can you get away with your love? It might be a Saturday afternoon in your bedroom or an hour in a hammock in the backyard; someplace away from the TV, computer, or iPod. Turn off your cell. God sometimes speaks to us in a whisper—a whisper that can be drowned out very easily. All it takes is the buzzing of an incoming text to interrupt your time with Jesus.

Are you willing to invest your heart and time this way? If so, where can you go that is quiet and undisturbed? When can you do this?

 # PRIVATE WHISPERS

It's also important for you to get quiet because he wants to whisper to you privately. There are words he has to say that he doesn't want to shout; words just for your ears. Think of a couple in love. Do they want to spend every moment of their time together surrounded by tons of people?

Cadillac Mountain is the highest point on the eastern seaboard in the United States; I experienced it just as the sun was setting. The purples and pinks mixed with the blues of the spring sky as the sun tucked its way behind the jagged peaks. Peaceful. Quiet. What was I surrounded by? Couples.

All over the mountain peak were couples whispering, snuggling. Doing what couples do. I wasn't alone either. Here, I was with my love, Jesus. He was brushing a beautiful painting for me in the dusky sky and I was taking it all in! That's why we need to get alone and get quiet with Jesus. He wants to whisper words of love to us too.

His whisper may be different for each one of us. Have you heard of love languages? In his book *The Five Love Languages*, Gary D. Chapman defines them as words of affirmation, quality time, receiving gifts, acts of service, and physical touch. The author talks about how each one of us gives and receives love in different ways—ways that often fall into these five categories. Understanding these different approaches can help us to understand ourselves and others. You can find out what your love language is by taking a quiz at www.5lovelanguages.com. (I know you love taking quizzes!)

Your love language is the way that you perceive love best. One of the ways I receive love is through gifts. (I mean, who doesn't want to receive gifts?!) God knows this about me and he knows I feel closest to him outside in his creation; it is his gift to me! Being in God's creation clears my mind and inspires me to focus on him.

> **I HAVE SEEN WHAT GLORIES OF CLIMATE, OF SUMMER MORNINGS AND EVENINGS, OF MIDNIGHT SKY. . . . ALL I HAVE SEEN TEACHES ME TO TRUST THE CREATOR FOR ALL I HAVE NOT SEEN.**
>
> —Ralph Waldo Emerson, "Immortality"

He Speaks to Me

Maybe in addition to speaking through his Word, he speaks to you through powerful music, inspirational poetry, or moving works of art. God can use anything he created! The Bible is his primary source, but he wants to use all of his creation. My good friend Carol is an amazing artist. When she has a clean canvas, she turns on worship music, asking Jesus to speak to her. As she worships, she mixes her strokes with vibrant colors. I have four of her works of art reminding me of Jesus' message of love!

He can also speak through other followers of Christ. I have had friends point out when my priorities seemed out of place. Another time a friend encouraged me to start using my gifts to serve in church. Just be sure that what they say is the same as what the Bible says. Jesus would never, ever say anything that is contrary to his Word.

In what ways have you begun to recognize God's love whispers? What has he been saying to you?

 # HOW BAD DO I WANT IT?

When it comes to hearing Jesus speak to you, ask yourself these questions: How bad do I want it? How bad do I want him? Hearing from him is not going to come easy, nor will it be free. Jesus explains this through a story in Matthew 13:44: "The kingdom of heaven is like treasure hidden in a field. When a man found it, he hid it again, and then in his joy went and sold all he had and bought that field."

WE HAVE AS MUCH OF JESUS AS WE WANT.
—Kathleen Dillard

In order to get the treasure, the man had to sell everything he had to get it. In order to get the treasure of hearing Jesus speak, we need to give up something valuable too. Our time.

I'm sure some days it seems like it's impossible to get more than five minutes alone with God, but if we want a truly deep relationship with him, we are going to have to spend a significant amount of time with him. Think about your best friend. Do you take just five minutes a day for her? If you did, she'd be so mad! The best way to develop great friendships is to spend large amounts of unhurried time together. The same is true with this friend. He doesn't want us to squeeze in time for him. He wants our time and our full attention.

Jesus practiced this in his relationship with his Father. He didn't wait until he was stressed out or

MY DIARY
February 2 (age fourteen): "In order to be on the youth board at church, Pastor Rich makes us fill in a report. We have to pray and read our Bible every day for thirty minutes. Hard, but really good for me."

He Speaks to Me

when his world was falling apart to spend time with him. He knew that God was his source of strength and encouragement.

FINDING A TIME AND PLACE

For many, the best time of the day to meet with Jesus is in the morning, when we can invite him to come and lead us. Talking to him is a great way to start the day. Mark 1:35 tells us: "Very early in the morning, while it was still dark, Jesus got up, left the house and went off to a solitary place, where he prayed."

I start before my feet ever hit the floor. He will often encourage me with a thought or a verse for something I might face that day. (You never know—those bad hair days can show up unannounced!) You can chat with him anytime, anywhere: while brushing your teeth, straightening your hair, walking to the bus stop, going on a run, playing your guitar, shooting hoops. Where and when do you converse with your friends? Talk with him there and then as well! He's your friend.

> *Because of the Lord's great love we are not consumed,*
> *for his compassions never fail.*
> *They are new every morning;*
> *great is your faithfulness.*
> *I say to myself, "The Lord is my portion;*
> *therefore I will wait for him."*
> *The Lord is good to those whose hope is in him,*
> *to the one who seeks him;*
> *it is good to wait quietly*
> *for the salvation of the Lord.*
> —Lamentations 3:22-26

His Revolutionary Love

I can hear some of you saying, "There is no way. I am barely able to wake up for my first class, let alone get up even earlier to read my Bible!" I hear you! Mornings are tough. You and the snooze button are best buds. If there is just no way it's going to happen for you in the morning, find the *same time* each day that you can meet with God. This will help you to be more consistent. If you had a regular chat time set up with your latest crush, you wouldn't miss it, would you? The love of your lifetime wants a date with you every day. Are you going to stand him up?

After all, your time with him is not all about you. Think about this picture: I loved hanging out with L.I.G.H.T., my small group of high school girls. I always looked forward to our time together. One Thursday, I spent a lot of time getting ready for them to come over. I built a fire in the fireplace and whipped up snacks. Four o'clock came and went.

THE LOVE OF YOUR LIFETIME WANTS A DATE WITH YOU EVERY DAY.

At 4:15 I started calling people. I soon found out that since it was a day off school, they had all forgotten our group meeting. I was bummed—so disappointed! I really wanted to hang out with them.

Trying not to pout, a thought popped into my head of a scene earlier in my day. I had awoken at 5:30 AM. Thinking it was time to get up, I headed to the shower. When I saw the clock, I remembered it wasn't a school day, so I could sleep an hour later. A second thought followed: "You could spend this time with the Lord." But instead of going with that idea, I rationalized, "I'm tired—I'll just pray in bed." Of course, I did what came naturally. I crawled right back into bed and immediately fell asleep!

He Speaks to Me

As this scene replayed in my head, I realized that I had disappointed Jesus, just like the girls had left me disappointed.

GET STARTED

When we begin something new, it can be like the start of a race. Sprinters take off at top speed . . . for a very short distance. We sometimes do the same with our plans for spending time with God. We start out saying "I am going to read my Bible every day for thirty minutes." Or "I'm going to read my Bible in a year." When we fall short, we figure we might as well quit.

Don't quit. Become consistent—even if it is for five minutes a day. I just stopped and read Genesis 1, the first chapter in the Bible. You know how long it took? Three minutes and ten seconds! We can all find three minutes and ten seconds to get started, right?

But where to start? That's not so hard. Just choose one book in the Bible. The Gospel of John is a great one to start with. It is the fourth book in the New Testament. Try reading a few verses each day. As you read, ask yourself two questions: Who is Jesus and what does he have to say to me? Jot down your answers somewhere where you won't lose them.

Let's try this plan out right now. Find the first verse of the first chapter of John. Are you there yet? OK, so read it: "In the beginning was the Word, and the Word was with God, and the Word was God."

Wow, this one looks deep. And it is. But it is not so deep that we can't figure out what God is saying. Dig in.

"In the beginning was the Word." In the beginning of what?

Write your answer. "Was the Word." What does that mean? See how *Word* is capitalized? It is a proper noun—a name. In this case, it's the name of a person (which becomes pretty clear as you read further along in this chapter). The person is Jesus; he is the Word.

So, for your entry for this Bible time you could write: "One of Jesus' names is the Word and he was at the very beginning of everything."

John goes on to say "and the Word was with God." So, Jesus and God were together at creation? Cool! "And the Word was God." Hold on! He was with God and he *was* God? Yep. He was God, because Jesus, God, and the Spirit of God make up the three-fold personality of God.

You might write: "Jesus was at creation because he has always been. He has always been because he is God." There! You did it!

Reading *this* book, the one in your hand, is also a great start. It is full of Scripture, but reading books about Jesus is not the same as reading the Bible. You have to read the Bible for yourself. Let's say your best friend often tells another friend stuff she likes about you. That friend then writes it down and gives you the note. Would that note thrill you or would you rather hear it directly from your best friend? Books are great, but make sure that you are also getting the real thing firsthand.

Having a friend or a group of friends to hold us accountable to our plans can be just what we need. Laurli shared this:

It wasn't until I got into L.I.G.H.T. (a small group whose name stands for Love Ignited Girls Hang Tight) and started spending more time with God that I really started to get it. Having a mentor and a group of girls who were growing and passionate helped so much.

Another girl I knew, Katelynn (nineteen), said she had been a Christian a really long time, but it wasn't until she joined L.I.G.H.T. and started reading her Bible regularly that she "really started to get it."

So what if you don't have a group like L.I.G.H.T. anywhere near you? Start your own group. It can be just you and a friend, you and a sibling, you and a parent, or you and anyone who will listen.

Don't be surprised if sometimes you get discouraged; that's normal. Don't quit. Just like in a friendship, sometimes you talk a lot and sometimes not as much, but that doesn't change the fact that you are still friends.

> *As you start (or continue, if you've already been doing this) reading your Bible and praying, do you feel God responding or does it seem as though he has been quiet? What messages from God's Word have meant the most to you so far?*

Karly, age sixteen, shared that when she thought she wasn't getting anywhere in following Christ, she gave up. Then she found out that by not following Christ, she lost herself. (She began making choices that would allow her to fit in with other people.) She didn't like the person she was becoming until she turned back to Christ again.

There really is nothing greater than hearing from Jesus each day through his Word, during prayer, and through our love languages. Learn the art of listening; it's well worth it! Learning to listen has saved me from some big mistakes as well as led me to some of the best things in my life. I want that for you too!

> *You will pray to him, and he will hear you,*
> *and you will fulfill your vows.*
> *What you decide on will be done,*
> *and light will shine on your ways.*
> —Job 22:27, 28

Connection

Make a connection with the one who wants you more than anything. Pray:

Jesus, I haven't really thought enough about you speaking to me as a friend. Help me to be

disciplined enough to come to you each day and
teach me to hear you in all of the ways that you long
to speak to me. Amen.

Radical Pursuits

Look at your schedule. When can you get alone with Jesus? Once you have figured out that time, make a commitment that for the next two weeks you will spend five minutes with him each day. If you are already doing that, great! Add five more. Just make sure to be consistent and write out each day what you are learning about Jesus and what he is saying to you.

When you spend time with him, ask God to speak to you and then be quiet for five minutes. This might be really hard! After the five minutes, write down a few points on what you heard. Don't get discouraged! Listening takes discipline; you can do it!

Tell someone you know about your commitment—like your mom or youth leader. Ask that person to hold you accountable. It's going to be great to hear what God has to say!

His Path for Me

CHAPTER ~ 4

I Need Him

*"But God will never forget the needy;
the hope of the afflicted will never perish."*

—Psalm 9:18

*I*f he were a cartoon, steam would be shooting out of the top of his head. His frustration boils over. Sliding up to the kitchen counter, sixteen-year-old Zach blurts out his issue: *"Girls drive me crazy! Why, when you're going out, do they constantly want you to call, text, or hang out?"*

Hmmm . . . how do I explain this one? I grab a couple of empty glasses on the counter: "I'd like to introduce you to two friends of mine, Zach. This one is Lexie and the other is Zoe." (Yes, I've just named two empty glasses. But keep reading anyway.) I then go on to explain to Zach how these two glasses, I mean girls, operate.

"Lexie wakes up each day, like many of us, feeling empty. She hits the alarm clock, straightens her hair, grabs breakfast, and heads for the bus. When she gets to school, her latest crush comments, 'Hey Lex, you look great today.' Lexie feels great; her heart fills up. That's all it takes."

EMPTY AGAIN, WHAT DOES SHE DO NOW?

Turning on the faucet, I stick the glass I've named Lexie under the stream of water, partially filling the empty glass. "Receiving an A on her algebra test fills her even more," I say, filling the glass up to the top. "After school, the callback list for the musical is posted—she wasn't chosen. All her great feelings go down the dark drain." I pour all the water out. "Empty again, what does she do now? She goes back to what she knows, back to Facebook, texting, music, sports, guys, friends—you, Zach. Whatever it takes to make her feel good, loved, and valued again."

I grab the other glass. "Zoe too wakes up in the morning feeling a little empty, but first thing, she spends time with Jesus. She reads the love letters he's written her, her Bible, mulling over his words again and again until they are deep within her heart. As he whispers words of love through the verses, she whispers words of love to him in prayer." I slip the empty glass under the stream of water from the faucet until the glass is filled to the top. "Now Zoe's day may look a lot like Lexie's—she looks great and aces a test too, making her feel good. These happy events add to her already full heart." As I allow the water from the faucet to just keep flowing, the glass spills over. "And you know what? All the great stuff in Zoe's heart pours out onto those close to her! Now, bad things will happen in Zoe's day—just like in Lexie's." I empty the glass. "But she knows where to go to get filled again. Back to Jesus, where she feels valued, loved, treasured. And the more she fills herself with him, the harder it will get for her to feel empty."

Zach stares at the two glasses. I'm sure he'll still get frustrated with "Lexie," but I see he understands the problem better now.

> *Satisfy us in the morning with your unfailing love,*
> *that we may sing for joy and be glad all our days.*
> *—Psalm 90:14*

I've been a Lexie. I've felt that roller coaster of emotion take me up with the excitement of a new crush and bring me plummeting down with rejection. I'd run to my best friend with every bit of news, good or bad. Though my friend tried to make me feel better, often I just felt worse. (She didn't have boyfriend problems, so she couldn't relate!) Other times I would lie in the dark, music thumping through my brain, hoping the throbbing lyrics would make me feel better. If not, chocolate was my last resort.

Do you know anyone like Lexie? A girl who runs to Facebook, texting, sports, food, guys—anywhere but to the one person who truly can make her feel valued, loved, treasured? Are you that girl?

Where do you run when you feel bad or down?

SOOTHING PSALMS

Trying to find someone who can relate to your feelings? Try browsing Psalms. The writer of many of these songs, King David, felt it all: joy, disappointment, humiliation, excitement, sadness. You'll find a perfect fit!

 ## HE COMPLETES ME

We hear about completion everywhere. Radio songs blare out our need to feel completed: "I can't breathe without you, but I have to" (from Taylor Swift, "Breathe"). Movies have whole plots based around the guy and girl getting together. (If they don't, we think it's a bad movie!) We can't get away from this sense of being completed by a guy.

God designed us with this need—this longing for love. But he created us to be satisfied in him. Matthew 5:48 says, "Be perfect, therefore, as your heavenly Father is perfect." You may be thinking, "Great! One more thing I can't possibly do—be perfect! As if life's not hard enough." But Susie Shellenburger, editor of *Susie Mag*, explains it this way: "In this context, the Greek word for *perfect* isn't determined by behavior. Christ isn't telling us that we have to be perfect humans—that's impossible. He's using the word *perfect* to describe being whole with our heavenly Father. God wants to perfect your heart! He wants to make you complete! He wants your wholeness to be found in him" (*Raising a Spiritually Strong Daughter* [Grand Rapids: Bethany House, 2009], 11).

We were created to be complete, but being complete can come from only one place—Jesus. You see, being needy isn't necessarily bad. Being needy can cause us to run to Jesus to find true joy, just like Zoe did.

What is true joy? Let's start with what it is not. Temporary happiness. Happiness can be an emotional high, but short-lived. Jesus describes his joy as *full*. Picture an ice cream sundae (something that brings me much temporary happiness!). Not one

> **TEAM JESUS**
>
> Have you read *New Moon*? Do you remember the emptiness and pain Bella felt when Edward was gone? Bella's heart began to feel complete in only one place—Edward's presence. First Corinthians 13:10 says that when "completeness comes, what is in part disappears." Where does your completeness come from?

I Need Him

of those puny ones from a fast-food place with two microscopic scoops and a dab of hot fudge. No way! This sundae has six

WHAT IS TRUE JOY?

scoops—it hardly fits in the bowl. Half a jar of hot fudge comes next, spilling over the edge. Top it off with whipped cream six inches high. That's the stuff I'm talking about—full.

Daily talking, consulting, crying, laughing, and dreaming with Jesus brings fullness in life, completion. I'm not saying life will not have pain and tough stuff in it—it will. Jesus said we will have trials and pain. It does mean his joyful peace will be within us, even when the bad stuff of life comes.

Pastor Steven Furtick made this statement, "My joy is not determined by what happens TO me, but what Christ is doing IN me and THROUGH me." Let me say that again: "My joy is not determined by what happens to me, but what Christ is doing in me and through me" (from the Joy Genome sermon series). The same applies with me feeling complete. My completion is not determined by what happens to me or even how I feel. My completion is determined by what Christ has done for me and is doing through me.

 ## MORE THAN ICING!

Have you ever gone to a wedding and stood in line for a piece of cake? What if, when you reached the server, she slid her pretty knife across those delicate sugar roses, serving you only the icing? *Psycho*—that's what you'd think. (Unless you are some kind of icing freak.)

Icing is not meant to be served alone! The cake is the substance of this yummy treat (especially when it's chocolate cake with chocolate frosting)!

Jesus is the cake, or the substance, of this life. He is everything. When he becomes *your* everything, the other good things in this life become icing on the cake! Success in sports, great grades, college scholarships, and making memories with our friends are all added bonuses; they make life better, but they only truly make life the best it can be if we are first filled in our hearts by Jesus.

Don't get me wrong; we both know we want those extras in life. Jesus wants to bring the icing to our lives as well. We find this expressed in Psalm 103:2-5: "Praise the Lord, my soul, and forget not all his benefits . . . who satisfies your desires with good things." Sometimes, though, we get confused. We try to have just the icing. Maybe we put things such as boyfriends, being part of a supercool group of friends, our family, or success in school in the first-place slot in our lives. When we try to find our happiness in these things alone, it just doesn't "taste" right. It doesn't satisfy us completely, or even worse, if it doesn't work out, we feel even emptier than we did before.

> *And I pray that you, being rooted and established in love, may have power, together with all the Lord's holy people, to grasp how wide and long and high and deep is the love of Christ, and to know this love that surpasses knowledge—that you may be filled to the measure of all the fullness of God.*
> —Ephesians 3:17-19

I Need Him

The Lord tells us he wants to fill every need we have. Zephaniah 3:17 says he is always with us. He takes great delight in us. We make him sing; he's so crazy about us! His perfect love quiets the girl drama, bringing his peace. His love moves my heart from stirring to settling—a place of comfort instead of confusion.

That place of comfort and completion comes when he has all of us.

Has anyone ever told you to "Give your heart to Jesus" or "Invite him into your life"? These phrases can leave a person with a sense that Jesus is an add-on or that he just wants part of us. We may begin to think Jesus + X = the Good Life (you fill in the blank—good grades, good times, good friends).

Look up John 14:6. What does Jesus say that he is?

> I came so they can have real and eternal life, more and better life than they ever dreamed of.
> —John 10:10 (*The Message*)

Satan, the enemy of our relationship with Jesus, really tries to distract us from realizing that Jesus is everything. He wants us to look to other things for happiness because he knows they will eventually let us down, leaving us empty. He wants us to eat the icing. He tried to pull off this same deception with Jesus.

In Matthew 4, Jesus headed out to the desert for some time with his Father. That's when Satan stepped in: "Come on—show them what you're made of!" Satan appealed to the part of Jesus that would want to be important, powerful, significant. Satan does the same with us. "You're the best actress in the school—you deserve that part." "You're prettier than his current girlfriend. You can get him to ask you out!" "You are a much stronger Christian. Aren't you glad you are not like *her?*"

When our need to feel loved and valued is not filled by Jesus, that need becomes a force of destruction in our lives. Satan knows what buttons to push to send us looking in the wrong places for our hearts to be filled. This need may show up in our lives in strange ways—masks for the real problem of an empty heart. Have you ever met a girl who seems to be mean for no apparent reason? Maybe she doesn't feel loved. Ever crossed paths with a beautiful girl who allows boys to use her? Chances are she feels empty. Do you ever look at your own life and think *Why do I care so much what they think?* I bet it is because you want to be liked by others. Jesus can fill all of those needs.

Sometimes, I still struggle. I hear all around me that I need something to validate me. Nineteen book rejections; that's how many times I heard no. Believe me, it can bring a girl down! During that time, my head would say, "You're not a good writer; no one will ever

> **MY DIARY**
> March 26 (age seventeen): "At my voice lesson after school with Miss B., I started crying. I'm afraid of the all-state competition on Saturday. I'm so scared; I don't want to fail! I need the Lord to teach me to sing for him."

I Need Him

publish you." I had to come to the place where my value wasn't determined by what I did; my value is found in Jesus!

 I NEED HIM TO FORGIVE ME

Popularity, respect, admiration, and esteem—we all want these things. Sometimes too much. Clamoring to be liked, we might find ourselves compromising our beliefs and convictions to gain approval, which often leads to actions that offend God. Lisa Bevere says it this way: "Dreams change to nightmares when we attempt to meet valid needs in invalid and inappropriate ways" (*Kissed the Girls and Made Them Cry* [Nashville: Thomas Nelson, 2002], 12).

When we offend God, we need to confess that sin. We need to recognize where we have gone wrong so we can avoid taking that path again. If we don't take the time to stop and think about this, we might just end up doing the same thing again. Doing something wrong in order to feel right. Trying to get filled up from empty sources.

MY DIARY
May 10 (age nineteen): "The Lord showed me that I wanted to use Greg to make me feel valuable and attractive and I wanted my friends to see that I was valuable to someone. That is so wrong. I need to change and turn around. I'm valuable because Jesus desires me."

Sin can also cause more emptiness inside us. Psalm 38:3, 4 gives us a picture of this empty feeling: "There is no soundness in my bones because of my sin. My guilt has overwhelmed me like a burden too heavy to bear." When we do something wrong, the guilt of that action can eat away at us. That leaves us with a hole that we once again need to fill up.

We need his forgiveness. It's only his forgiveness that can patch the holes inside us, making us complete again. We need to repent. Repentance is saying "I am sorry" (and meaning it), asking for forgiveness, and turning the other direction.

God won't hold your sin against you. He won't keep reminding you of the wrong you did in the past. Hebrews 8:12 (*NLT*) reminds us, "I will forgive their wickedness, and I will never again remember their sins." We can trust him to do just that!

I NEED TO TRUST HIM

Have you ever had a friend betray you, a parent blame you, or a boyfriend cheat on you? If so, you may feel uneasy about trusting Jesus. Maybe a painful experience has left you scared of vulnerability and opening up. No one wants her heart crushed!

You can trust him completely. Ask him to help you to be vulnerable with your faults, pains, and struggles. He can answer honest prayers: "Lord, help me to want to know you!" His safe, steady heart gives us reason to risk giving everything important to his care. He is the best Father you could ever know. He always will do what is best for you.

Write out one of my favorite verses, Isaiah 49:16.
What stands out to you from this verse?

THE KING OF THE UNIVERSE IS CONSTANTLY THINKING OF YOU.

He writes your name on his hand. How amazing! The King of the universe is constantly thinking of you.

His love reminds me of the fountain in my backyard. The flow of water never ends; it spills over the gray, mossy shelf into the pond below twenty-four hours a day, seven days a week, and three hundred sixty-five days a year. I don't have to turn it on, push the water over the edge, or worry about it drying up. Continuous, faithful, and never ending. As your relationship with Jesus grows and deepens, his love becomes a fountain within you, filling in the deepest parts of your heart. Twenty-four hours a day, seven days a week, three hundred and sixty-five days a year, Jesus is a continual place of solace and abundance. His perfect love flows into us, filling our hearts.

If you will invest in this relationship and give him everything, you will never be disappointed. He won't use you, dump you, cheat on you, or forget you. His love is perfect. Perfect for filling you up. Perfect for you.

 *Connection*

Make a connection with the one who wants you more than anything. Pray:

Jesus, make me like Zoe—filled up and completed by you. Every time I run to something or someone, help me recognize I'm running to the wrong things. Help me run to you! Amen.

Radical Pursuits

Below I have listed my favorite verses. Pick one to memorize this week. Write it in your journal and memorize it with another person. Put it everywhere you can: your calendar, your screen saver, your mirror, your dashboard . . . any place where you can see it and read it often.

> *Keep me as the apple of your eye;*
> *hide me in the shadow of your wings.*
> —Psalm 17:8

> *Can a mother forget the baby at her breast*
> *and have no compassion on the child she has borne?*
> *Though she may forget,*
> *I will not forget you!*
> *See, I have engraved you on the palms of my hands;*
> *your walls are ever before me.*
> —Isaiah 49:15, 16

> *See what great love the Father has lavished on us, that we should*
> *be called children of God! And that is what we are! The reason the*
> *world does not know us is that it did not know him.*
> —1 John 3:1

CHAPTER ~ 5

I Go After Him

*"Come near to God and
he will come near to you."*

—James 4:8

hink, Sarah! Where did you put it? Borrowing her sister's camera for her choir trip seemed a good idea. Now Maggie wanted it. Panicking, Sarah racked her brain. *Where did I put that thing?!* The hot tears started to flow as she desperately scoured her room for a glimpse of that red camera. Since it was Maggie's Christmas gift from their parents, Sarah knew she better look and look hard until that camera was found.

Ever been there? Misplace something important? your cell? iPod? a special note from a special someone? Did you just decide that you'd get around to looking for it later? No way! Everything came to a halt until your treasure was found.

I want my relationship with Jesus to be like that. I want him to be the thing that I put everything else aside for—the most important thing. Sounds easy, but making him my biggest deal sometimes isn't.

 ## GET READY

Jesus told a story in Matthew about some girls who had a problem similar to mine. Check out Matthew 25:1-13 (*The Message*):

> God's kingdom is like ten young virgins who took oil
> lamps and went out to greet the bridegroom. Five were
> silly and five were smart. The silly virgins took lamps,
> but no extra oil. The smart virgins took jars of oil to feed
> their lamps. The bridegroom didn't show up when they
> expected him, and they all fell asleep. In the middle of the
> night someone yelled out, "He's here! The bridegroom's
> here! Go out and greet him!" The ten virgins got up and
> got their lamps ready. The silly virgins said to the smart

ones, "Our lamps are going out; lend us some of your oil." They answered, "There might not be enough to go around; go buy your own." They did, but while they were out buying oil, the bridegroom arrived. When everyone who was there to greet him had gone into the wedding feast, the door was locked. Much later, the other virgins, the silly ones, showed up and knocked on the door, saying, "Master, we're here. Let us in." He answered, "Do I know you? I don't think I know you." So stay alert. You have no idea when he might arrive.

The silly girls were excited about meeting the party giver and in their excitement, they just took off. A celebration was going on; they had to be in on it. Problem was, they didn't get ready first. (Can you imagine going to a party without getting ready?!)

ALWAYS A BRIDESMAID

Five great movies about weddings.
1. *27 Dresses*
2. *My Best Friend's Wedding*
3. *Runaway Bride*
4. *Bride Wars*
5. *My Big Fat Greek Wedding*

Think of it like a group of girls heading out to a huge back-to-school bonfire at a friend's lake house. It's a bit of a drive, so they decide to all pile in the car together. No one bothers to check the gas gauge. Halfway there, the tank runs dry.

They wanted to be where the fun was happening, but no one prepared. They didn't do what it took to make sure they got there. It's kind of like the girls in Jesus' story; they ran out of fuel in their oil-burning lamps before the party even got rolling.

I Go After Him

The second group of girls was also excited, but they prepared first. They put oil in their lamps so that they could be at the bash all night long. In this story Jesus was contrasting two types of people. There are those who know about Jesus—maybe they even call themselves Christians—but they don't spend time investing in a relationship with him. A girl might say, "Yeah, I'm a Christian; my parents are. We go to church; I attend youth group. Every summer I even go to church camp. I believe it. Yeah, I'm a Christian." But that's where it ends. There is nothing in her life that shows that she's been transformed by the revolutionary love of Jesus.

Contrast her to the girl who does what it takes to know Jesus. Like the wise girls in Jesus' story, this girl spends time with Jesus one-on-one. She wants him and his love so much, she invests in her relationship with him. Praying, reading the Bible, and learning to listen to what his voice sounds like are each a really big deal in her life. She is finding out how to return his revolutionary, radical love; she's going after him. Even when it's not exciting, she keeps pursuing him. She doesn't give up.

Sarah had to turn her bedroom upside down until she found Maggie's camera. Even when she didn't find it right away, she kept looking. Jesus wants us to pursue him the same way—setting aside other things in order to spend time getting to know him better.

 ## SEEKING GOD

Did you ever play hide-and-seek? When you were "it" you had to look and look and look until you found each person. You didn't casually stroll around the yard hoping you might just happen to run into someone. Instead, you had to look hard for each player—especially if you were playing in the dark!

That's how Jesus says we are to seek him. Jeremiah 29:12-14 describes it this way: "Then you will call on me and come and pray to me, and I will listen to you. You will seek me and find me when you seek me with all your heart. 'I will be found by you,' declares the Lord."

YOU WILL SEEK ME AND FIND ME WHEN YOU SEEK ME WITH ALL YOUR HEART.

Seek isn't a passive verb. Seeking takes effort. Going to church with your family, being part of a Christian organization at school, or going to youth group isn't the end of seeking. Volunteering in the church nursery isn't seeking either—even if you do come out each week with baby spit all over your shirt.

Seeking involves learning about who he is, what he is like, and then being intentional about becoming like him.

According to Deuteronomy 4:29, how should we seek him?

The words *all your heart and all your soul* depict a relationship that is intense. To me that phrase describes a love that is the deepest kind. That type of deep love doesn't develop fast. This is no quickie relationship.

If you believed what many movies and TV shows feed us, you'd think today's romances were like the drive-up window at your favorite fast-food joint: quick and cheap. Girl meets boy, boy takes girl home, girl sleeps with boy, boy and girl move in together. There is no "becoming." One night you are strangers and single, the next you are a couple. This relationship is not like that!

When I was eighteen I left home to go to a ministry training school. Our counselors strongly encouraged us not to date while we were in the program. This was a season in our lives to focus on our relationship with Jesus. I had a really hard time with this when the love of my life happened to come along at that same time! (I'll give you the whole story in a chapter to come, I promise.)

MY DIARY

August 11 (age eighteen): "The Lord revealed to me that wanting a relationship with Greg right now was an idol in my life—something I wanted more than I wanted him. How do I steer my heart clear from deception? By focusing on God."

What appeared to be the best thing ever could have been a huge distraction in my life, a derailment of my focus. My counselor reminded me that the kind of relationship that I wanted to have with Jesus required my full attention. She was right. I chose to focus only on Jesus during that season; that decision has made all the difference in my life! That time I spent focused on just Jesus and me gave me a foundation for a lifelong love with him.

 GETTING STRONGER

The time we spend pursuing Jesus and listening to him gives our relationship with him strength and depth. Have you ever observed an older couple that has been married forever? After being together for fifty years, do they talk of divorce when they get in a fight? No, that would be weird! After that much time together, they have learned to get through stuff—big and small. Now think about you or your friend's last crush. One little fight and it was over. There was no strength whatsoever because the relationship was shallow and based only on emotions.

That is what you and Jesus need to develop together—strength that comes through experience and history. This history of knowing and trusting him is exactly what you will gain when you pursue him. History with Jesus will carry your relationship no matter what comes! Seeing him at work in your life, seeing his faithfulness, will help you trust him with the future.

Where do you start? Begin pursuing him by putting what you learn into action. Trust him to work out relationships that drive you crazy, giving you wisdom on how you need to respond. Ask for direction on big decisions in your life and follow what he shows you. Make a choice to praise him, instead of complaining, even when life stinks.

The more you see and experience Jesus' faithfulness in your life, the easier it will be to trust him. The part of you that feels driven to fix things will begin to turn to him to fix things. Your relationship with him will become more consistent and less like a roller coaster. You will develop the discipline to keep running toward him, no matter what.

Sometimes when you spend time with him you might feel like this: "I showed up. I prayed, I worshipped, and I read your Word. Where were you?" He was there. Remember that your feelings can trick you. Try not to get discouraged—even those times when you feel like you're talking to air will pay off. He sees your faithfulness and discipline.

Hang in there. The more you invest in him, the more you will see him working through your life. Some friends will turn to drugs or drinking for a good time or to forget their troubles, but you will have a purpose. While others can't seem to figure out what they should do with their lives, you can have a sense of direction and know why you were created. When others seem to be lost, you will know where, and to whom, you belong.

THE ONE WHO WOULD KNOW GOD MUST GIVE TIME TO HIM.

—A. W. Tozer, *The Divine Conquest*

It doesn't mean life will be easy. Some of the times when I have been pursuing God the most, life has seemed to actually get harder! During these times, I've learned to keep on pursuing Jesus. I've realized that love will take me way further in my relationship with him than following rules or feelings ever can.

Intimacy with Jesus does not come fast or easy—it takes determination. Have you ever had a complete blowup with your best friend? At that point, you either dropped your friendship or you worked through it. We need that same tenacity to work through things in our relationships with Christ. In 1 Peter 4:12, 13 (*The Message*), Peter wrote: "Friends, when life gets really difficult, don't jump to the conclusion that God isn't on the job. Instead, be glad that you are in the very thick of what Christ experienced. This is a spiritual refining process, with glory just around the corner."

One of the results of spending more time with Jesus is that our desire to obey grows stronger (overcoming our desire to rebel). Obedience then opens doors for blessings. I've seen this in my life. Doors such as a school placement opening up at just the right time and developing friends who are going in the same direction I am. God has opened doors for me to write and speak, which I love! And doors leading to a life that is full of joy and peace!

LET US NOT BECOME WEARY IN DOING GOOD.

Look at the words of encouragement Paul offered us in Galatians 6:9: "Let us not become weary in doing good, for at the proper time we will reap a harvest if we do not give up."

Name something that you have either wanted in the past or want now. What did you do or are you doing now to get that?

Some of the things that you might want are good grades, getting into a great college, getting assigned the solo in choir, or making it to the state competition in your sport. To reach any one of these, you need commitment, discipline, and time. It could possibly require more than you are doing now. But you expect it to be worth it all when you reach that goal.

Now contrast that feeling of accomplishment with how you feel when something is handed to you. It is nice, but it isn't the same. Isn't the thing that actually cost *you* something more valuable to you? Just like any of the goals you might have listed above, if you want to experience a deep level of intimacy with Jesus, it will cost you—time, energy, discipline, and vulnerability, among other things. Unlike those other goals, this one comes with a 100 percent guarantee that it will be worth the investment.

In his letter to the Philippians, Paul wrote this (3:7-9, *The Message*): "Yes, all the things I once thought were so important are gone from my life. Compared to the high privilege of knowing Christ Jesus as my Master, firsthand, everything I once thought I had going for me is insignificant—dog dung. I've dumped it all in the trash so that I could embrace Christ and be embraced by him."

Paul spelled out the cost. He said his desire to have Christ and for Christ to have all of him was so great that when you compared everything else in life to this great treasure, it was worthless garbage. (Only a little worse—"dog dung." Seriously gross!)

Think about the things you spend loads of time on, the things that take up a lot of your thoughts, text messages, or daydreams. What things are you

tempted to hang on to instead of letting go of to have a closer relationship with Jesus? What things have you desired or thought were very significant in the past that now seem not so valuable? What caused this change?

In Job 22:25, 26, in replying to Job, what does Eliphaz say God will be for him if he returns to him? What do you think he is saying here?

This relationship is not for the half-hearted. If you want to find him to be your everything, you have to give him your everything. That doesn't mean you are perfect, that you have all of your stuff together. It does mean that you are fully committed to follow him as he gives you the strength. We'll talk more about that in the next chapter.

Connection

Make a connection with the one who wants you more than anything. Pray:

Jesus, I don't want boring Christianity. I want passion. I want authenticity. I get how I need to go after you like you are coming after me. I want to be radical—a world changer. Give me strength, Jesus. Amen.

Radical Pursuits

Write a note to Jesus in your journal, or write it here. Be honest about your relationship with him. What is the next step for you to see your relationship deepen—for you to go after this radical love? If you are feeling frustration, tell him. If you need discipline, he gives that too. Ask him to make himself known to you in a way that you can see and understand.

You can write your note here.

CHAPTER ~ 6

I Honor Him

"We make it our goal to please him."

—2 Corinthians 5:9

*A**m I going to be all alone?* Samantha still clutched her phone. Michael had just ended the call with her, saying he didn't want to be friends anymore. He was heading down a different path than she was; experimenting with girls was the only thing on his mind. Samantha said she wasn't going that way. Michael's response: "I guess we can't be friends."

This is happening more and more to Samantha. Everywhere she turns, it's becoming apparent that her life is different. A small thing, like not joining in when a new girl is being made fun of, is now a big thing. Refusing to be mean to kids is noticed by others.

HONOR. PURITY. IT ISN'T JUST A SEX THING.

Samantha knows she is different; the love she receives from Jesus compels her. She just wants to honor God and be pure. Before now, she hadn't ever thought about what that really meant.

Honor. Purity. It isn't just a sex thing. It's a mind thing and a heart thing. A few years ago Hayley DiMarco wrote a wildly popular book, *Technical Virgin*. Books flew off the shelves—bought by girls dying to know "How far is too far?" But if they read the book, I think they found out they were asking the wrong question.

Being a technical virgin, a virgin in the most basic sense of the word, is not God's best. I was a virgin and proud of it. I was also the judgmental type—you know anyone who fits that description? "I would NEVER do THAT!" Yeah, *that* type. I felt sure I knew the answer to "How far is too far?" But the real question I should have been asking myself was "Am I honoring God in my life?"

His Revolutionary Love

Was I really pure? No, not always. Not by a long shot. You want to know one thing I really was? Prideful. Self-righteous too. I put myself above others. There were times when I wished I had the opportunity to do things that I knew were wrong. (I kept my boundaries really tight, not much room for temptation.) But when I did cross my own boundaries, I would find myself lying in my bed at night wishing I hadn't done what I said I wouldn't do. At other times, I wished for a conscience that wasn't so sensitive.

Madi, thirteen, talked about this kind of struggle: "*Knowing how much he loves me makes me feel like I am not alone—I have someone I can talk to. He helps me with the temptations I have: dressing inappropriately, gossiping, and things like that.*"

 ## HONOR HIM IN YOUR HEART

What I failed to see was that my tender conscience was a gift; it was a product from the time I spent with Jesus. He changed me. When we start to really understand this revolutionary, radical love, there are many different outcomes, purity being one of them. We begin to have a heart and will that honor God. This helps to shape our actions.

When I say the word *purity*, what do you think? Maybe you think "That doesn't describe me!" Notice the word is not *perfection*. *Perfection* and *purity* are not synonyms. Being pure, trying to grow a pure heart, doesn't mean you won't ever make any mistakes. It also isn't just about what you don't or will not do. Saying no to every bad thing won't guarantee you a pure heart. You have to work at it.

You have to work at not only keeping things out, but also putting the right things in.

Paul says purity on the outside comes from purity on the inside: "Everything is pure to those whose hearts are pure. But nothing is pure to those who are corrupt and unbelieving, because their minds and consciences are corrupted" (Titus 1:15, *NLT*). Those whose minds are not pure cannot be pure of heart; that's why their actions don't honor God.

But guess what! It's not all up to you, this stuff about keeping pure. In fact, you just can't do it by yourself. (Sigh of relief.) Proverbs 16 includes a few sayings that help us see the truth (vv. 2, 3):

> *All a person's ways seem pure to them,*
> *but motives are weighed by the Lord.*
> *Commit to the Lord whatever you do,*
> *and he will establish your plans.*

If you ask God for help to stay pure, he will help you. If you commit your heart to God, he will help you know how to honor him with it.

 # WHAT DOES HONOR LOOK LIKE?

One way of figuring out what it means to honor God is to look at the definition of *honor*. *Webster's Dictionary* says *to honor* means to "treat (someone) with admiration or respect." If you think about it long enough, I'm sure you can come up with one or several examples of people in your life to whom you show "admiration or respect." Maybe there is a teacher, a coach, a mentor, a pastor, a boss, or a team leader that you show respect to. Or maybe—shocker!—it's your mom or dad.

What does respect for one of the people mentioned above look like for you? How do you show respect?

Sometimes honor is shown by gifts given or offerings made to the person or thing to be honored. Proverbs 3:9 says, "Honor the LORD with your wealth, with the firstfruits of all your crops." But often, honoring God in the Bible involves actions, behaviors, and decisions that show a person is following God's will. Proverbs 14:31 says, "Whoever is kind to the needy honors God." But actions alone aren't good enough. Jesus quoted Old Testament Scripture when he gave the hypocritical Pharisees and teachers of the law a piece of his mind (Matthew 15:8): "'These people honor me with their lips, but their hearts are far from me.'"

I asked Kylie, age sixteen, what she thought it meant to honor God:

I think to honor God means to fully devote ourselves to him, in actions and in words. We should honor his Word by not only doing what it says, but following through with a cheerful attitude. Not as

I Honor Him

though we are being forced to. For me, it's most difficult in the area of relationships. I personally feel that God has called me to not date throughout my high school experience. Although I'm physically doing what he tells me to, I don't always follow through mentally, which is really what it's all about.

So showing respect to God means choosing every day to give him the best of what we have to offer, to do his will, and to make sure our hearts have the right motives. Showing him respect every day in the things we do and say can be one of the ways we worship Jesus. It's a way of demonstrating that he is the Lord of our lives—and our true love as well!

HEALTHY FEAR

My friend Annie loves softball. Sometimes we like to go to the batting cages together. Now when Annie gets in the batting cage, she knows exactly where to stand. She doesn't stand in the middle; she positions herself beside the plate. Annie has a healthy fear while she's in that batting cage. She's smart enough to know that the pitching machine throws balls sixty miles per hour. If she is in the wrong place at the wrong time, she's going to get creamed! Her knowledge of the machine is what gives her fear. And her fear of the machine is good; it keeps her from getting hurt.

Proverbs 9:10 says that the fear of the Lord is the beginning of wisdom. Fear of the Lord is the healthiest kind of fear. *Fear* here means reverence, respect. The Lord is the source of all wisdom. Having respect for him is the first step in gaining that wisdom. It's hard (sometimes impossible) to learn anything from someone you don't respect. God, the creator of the universe, the all-powerful, all-knowing King of kings commands our respect, our fear.

It is not too far off from Annie and her pitching machine. She fears the machine when it is in action because she knows what it can do. Her fear does not keep her from doing what she needs to do. In fact, the exact opposite is true. She goes on practicing hitting those balls. Her fear allows her to do what she needs to do, without getting injured by an incoming fast pitch.

That phrase "the fear of the Lord" or "the fear of God" often gets misused. People talk about putting the fear of God into someone. Or we might hear of people who say they have a fear of God, or a fear of church. But when people use these words that way, they are not talking about a reverence for God. They are talking about being afraid of something, and that something isn't even really God. It's usually something else—perhaps someone's misconceptions about God, or an experience with an unhealthy church or pastor, or some other person who has done them harm in the past.

We "fear" God, we respect him, because we know who he is and what he can do. This kind of fear does not keep us from being who we are. It does not keep us from doing what we need to do.

UNHEALTHY FEARS

1. Fear of pencils.
2. Fear of ice cream.
3. Fear of oxygen.

HEALTHY FEARS

1. Fear of venomous snakes.
2. Fear of drugs.
3. Fear of Mom/Dad before morning coffee.

I Honor Him

Instead, it gives us a key to wisdom. It lets us start to understand who God created us to be and what we are meant to do. Proverbs 9:11 says that "through wisdom your days will be many, and years will be added to your life." We all want to live a long time, don't we? Then we need to fear and honor God. His wisdom will keep us from getting hurt.

 ## ONE STEP LEADS TO ANOTHER

One choice to honor God, be it small or large, can lead to a life that honors God. A pure life.

On the flip side, one choice, be it small or large, made to dishonor God can lead to a messed-up life. Who comes to mind when I say "messed-up"? Do you picture a girl who has had an abortion or is unmarried and pregnant? Is it that guy doing drugs? Does someone you know have a reputation of letting guys use her? Has some boy turned his back on his family's faith to gain his independence? Maybe you think of a family member, a best friend, or maybe . . . you.

Whoever you are thinking of, how do you think that person ended up where he or she is today? Did he just wake up one morning and fall off the deep end? Did she eat something funny that changed her life? Probably not. It started when they didn't fear God—when they made one decision that seemed small, harmless.

One decision at a time, they failed to take into account whether or not they were honoring God. They didn't stop to ask "God, what is your will for my life?"

Instead, they stepped into the line of fire. "It's OK to go with

His Revolutionary Love

him just once. I know he's a 'bad boy,' but he's so cute." "I know that I talk that way on Facebook, but I would never actually do that stuff." "I can handle hanging out with them—it's not like anyone's going to force me to do what they do." String them all together and what do you have? A direct course heading where you don't want to go. It can happen to anyone.

The really cool thing is that the same is true for living a life that honors God. One small step toward honoring him, a step of obedience, leads to another. Eventually, this path leads to experiencing God's best for us.

Starting at a young age, I made deliberate choices to follow Jesus. Careful to choose friends who were heading in the same direction, I tried to avoid situations that were tempting. This included only dating guys who were Christ followers (for me, the absolute hardest choice). Other choices had to do with the music I did and didn't listen to and which movies and TV shows I watched. I wanted to follow Jesus with my decision on where I went to school once I had graduated from high school. I didn't get it right every time, but the love that Jesus had for me and I had for him motivated me to honor him.

My life is an example of the benefits of making choices to honor Jesus. I'm not bragging—I had a lot of help to make the choices I did. Our lives have so many choices. Will I marry and if so, who? What will I do with my life? For me, the benefits that came from making God-honoring choices include marrying a godly man that I had saved myself for, discovering the gifts Jesus has given me, getting to do what I love, and freedom from some of the pain and consequences that often follow poor decisions. One of the greatest benefits of a life that honors God is the lack of the burden of shame or regret to live with each day.

I asked Kari, twenty-eight, how understanding Jesus' love and choosing to honor him made a difference when she was in school:

> *I tried to honor God in everything I did, meaning having both a thankful heart and a willingness to do what he asked of me. As we mature and grow in relationship with our heavenly Daddy, we become increasingly more thankful for his everlasting love and for his constant protection and provision. . . . We show this by thanking him every day for his goodness and by obeying his Word. The things he asks us to do or not to do are, after all, for our own protection.*

NO SUCH THING AS LUCK

It is so great that we don't have to make hard choices alone. Jesus does not leave us on our own. Once we have accepted him, with the Holy Spirit living inside of us, we have the power to make God-honoring decisions. Don't underestimate his power. Making a decision to rely on his power can lead to amazing results!

You see, good lives don't just happen; fate has nothing to do with it. There is no such thing as luck. Wise Choices + the Power of the Holy Spirit = a Blessed Life. Notice that I didn't say a perfect life, but it is a life with God's goodness and joy in it.

Mariah knows about choices. At sixteen, she has decided she

wants to major in music. This is not going to be an easy task; she just started piano lessons! She's meeting with a vocal instructor weekly. Now she has found the hardest piano teacher in town, requiring her to practice forty-five minutes a day, five days a week. When I asked Mariah if she likes practicing, she responded, *"No, but it's what I need to do if I want to perform. It will be worth it."* Mariah has a goal; she's doing what it takes.

JESUS DOES NOT LEAVE US ON OUR OWN.

What are your goals? Is one of them honoring God? What are you doing to meet your goals?

 ## GOD-SIZED GOAL

In 2 Corinthians 5:9, Paul wrote to the Christians in the city of Corinth and told them, "We make it our goal to please [the Lord]." Knowing how to please God is not that complicated, but obedience can be. That is where the hard part comes in. Many of the choices

I Honor Him

we make to please God won't win us friends. Galatians 1:10 says, "Am I now trying to win the approval of human beings or of God? Or am I trying to please people? If I were still trying to please people, I would not be a servant of Christ."

The message is pretty clear. Much of the time, we're going to be faced with this question: Am I going to make choices that win my friends' approval or God's? Most likely it will not be both. The thing that makes these tough choices easier is knowing our God loves us so!

What are some of the choices you are faced with on a daily basis that give you the chance to choose whether or not to honor Jesus?

What do you want out of life?

" I want a life that is God's best for me."

" I want to marry a godly man and to serve God together."

" I want a life where financially I'm free and not in debt."

" I want to have true joy and be satisfied with living out my purpose."

Start with right choices—God-honoring decisions. Andy Stanley says in his book *The Principle of the Path,* "Ask yourself the question, 'What is the wise thing to do?'"

Get in the habit of asking yourself questions. How do you treat your little sister when she causes you to drop your straightener on your bare foot? What comes out of your mouth when your parents say no to the party? How about that guy in first period who's been texting you and you know is going to ask you out? Does he follow Jesus? How will you answer?

It's pretty simple. Honoring God comes down to finding out the answers to all these little questions (and some big ones). If you want God's best for you, you have to make choices that let you learn about what that is. If you want to marry a godly man, then date guys who follow Jesus. Find out what a godly man should be. If you want to stay out of debt, only buy what you can pay for. If you want to find true joy and be content, run to Jesus when you are hurting or happy. You'll develop a relationship with him that is not based on emotions, but one that is stable and leads to joy and purpose.

Simple, but not easy. The closer you are to Jesus, the easier honoring him will be. Ask the Spirit of God to help you.

Connection

Make a connection with the one who wants you more than anything. Pray:

In some ways this seems really hard, Jesus. I know I would really be different if I chose to live

life each day making choices that honor you. I want to do that. Empower me, Holy Spirit, to make one right choice at a time. Amen.

Radical Pursuits

Define areas of your life where you are making God-honoring decisions. Define areas of your life where you are not making God-honoring decisions.

Think about these actions you can take:

- Do you have issues with purity while on the Internet? Ask your parents to put a filter on your computer.
- Problems with boyfriend boundaries? If you are scared to talk to him, write him a letter saying exactly what you need to say.
- Questions about dressing modestly? Ask your mom or best friend to go through your closet with you, helping you to remove anything too short, too low, and too tight.
- Facebook temptations? Add your mom or youth leader as your "friend," asking them to hold you accountable about what you post online.

His Hopes for Me

CHAPTER ~ 7

We Protect Together

*"You are a garden locked up,
my sister, my bride;
you are a spring enclosed, a sealed fountain."*

—Song of Solomon 4:12

*I*t was the place to be. God had given our youth pastor great ideas to make our youth group the coolest place, and it grew like crazy. Even popular kids from our local schools came. That is where Shawna and Matt met. They both turned their lives over to Jesus; their excitement for him was infectious. Just like the rest of us, Shawna and Matt were in church every chance they got. At first, they hung out with our entire group. Then they became exclusive.

They started out just leaving a little bit before everyone else, so they could get to know each other better. Then they started missing an event here, a meeting there. Being together, alone, was more fun than being with a huge group. Besides, everyone else just seemed so immature. Before they knew it, they were alone all the time—church and their friends became a thing of the past.

So did their purity. Eventually, Shawna and Matt broke up. The intimacy they thought would bring them together actually drove them apart—leaving them with wounded and broken hearts.

Their story is a common one. It breaks Jesus' heart and mine too. His best for us is much greater. His is a story of love, not heartbreak. Check out this passage where this type of love is described (Song of Solomon 4:13-15, *The Message*):

> Dear lover and friend, you're a secret garden,
> a private and pure fountain.
> Body and soul, you are paradise,

a whole orchard of succulent fruits—
Ripe apricots and peaches,
oranges and pears;
Nut trees and cinnamon,
and all scented woods;
Mint and lavender,
and all herbs aromatic;
A garden fountain, sparkling and splashing,
fed by spring waters from the Lebanon mountains.

The Song of Solomon can be looked at in different ways. To some, it is a picture of the passionate love that occurs between a groom and his bride. To others, it is a poetic metaphor of the love of Christ for his bride, the church. It's good to keep both of these views in mind when reading the verses. It can also help us to consider the time and setting in which the words were written. Song of Solomon was probably composed sometime around 965 BC, and in a land where fruits and spices of the type mentioned in 4:13-15 would have been difficult to get—they were only for the wealthy and royalty.

Using these precious commodities to describe his love for his bride was a huge compliment. The bridegroom, representing Jesus, said the bride, representing you, is extremely valuable. That, my friend, is who you are—royalty. You are loved by the King! You are half of the royal couple!

The conversation between the bride and bridegroom continues in 4:16 with the bride calling to the groom to come and taste the choice fruits. Remember I mentioned that these fruits were exclusive, uncommon. These choice fruits represent the bride's unique purity; the thing she has saved exclusively for the king. Notice here that not just anyone was allowed to taste these choice fruits—only one. The king.

 ON GUARD

Enough with the fruits, let's get to the point! Sometimes in dating relationships conversations that are had, secrets that are shared, and physical contact that takes place are not good. Intimate actions such as these open the door that is meant to be opened only by a godly husband in the context of marriage. Physical and emotional intimacy are to be saved; your heart and mind and body are valuable. They are your treasures that you will share with the man you marry.

In chapter two of Song of Solomon, the bride passed on wise advice to her friends: "Oh, let me warn you . . . don't excite love, don't stir it up, until the time is ripe—and you're ready" (v. 7, *The Message*). Today she might have said, "Girl, don't let that crush get out of control. Wait until after 'I do.' Protect your heart."

GUARD YOUR HEART ABOVE ALL ELSE.

Stirred up. Isn't that what you feel when a guy starts paying attention to you? Your heart starts doing flip-flops. You do flip-flops to get his attention. These flip-flop actions often don't honor God. Maybe you dress for attention, talk impurely, or go places mentally or physically that head in the wrong direction.

As one loved by the King, you are precious to him. As a servant of the King, you are on guard. Proverbs 4:23 (*NLT*) says: "Guard your heart above all else, for it determines the course of your life." Pretty radical, right? But it's true—you'll never have a more important mission than this kind of guard duty. And no one else can do it for you. Not your mom, not your friends, and certainly not that hot guy in chemistry lab.

 PROTECT THE GUYS

What?? That's what you're probably saying when you read this heading. Why do I have to protect guys? Here's why. Look at this picture.

Can you complete this picture? Did you know exactly what to do? Your brain told you, right? The same is true with a guy's brain. They finish what has been started. If you leave half of your body undressed, a guy's brain automatically finishes the picture. If you flirt with words that create a certain image in his mind, he'll complete that image. And I hate to gross you out, but I'm not just talking about guys your age. The same goes for your teachers, coaches, and your friend's dad.

Here is what Joshua Harris, author of *Boy Meets Girl*, said: "Girls have no idea how difficult it is for a guy to look at you with purity in his heart when they choose to dress immodestly" (from an interview with Dannah Gresh for *And the Bride Wore*

White [Chicago: Moody Publishers, 2004]). As girls, we may have a hard time understanding what happens when you add a half-dressed girl plus an average male mind. This doesn't make guys perverts or animals; it makes them normal. They've got their own responsibilities to guard their thoughts and control their actions. But it is our responsibility not to trigger these thoughts by the outfits we put together—our responsibility is to protect them and ourselves as well.

Harris also pointed out that "girls face the temptation to pick out the shorter skirt in the closet because they know that it grabs the guy's attention." Have you ever experienced this power? power to turn heads in the parking lot or lure eyes in the hallway? Girl, guard your heart against desiring this type of attention. It is very normal for you to want attention, everyone wants to be wanted—to know that you are beautiful and someone loves to be near you. That need for attention is to be met by our radical lover, Jesus. You were created for his love and affection.

MY DIARY

July 28 (age nineteen): "Today Lisa, my counselor at school, corrected me for dressing immodestly. I know I still dress for attention. It made me cry because I knew she was right. I see how I place part of my identity on my looks."

Have you ever dressed for attention? If so, why did you do it?

Just like you, I like to look my best. But making a decision to dress in a way that is inappropriate is a very selfish decision. It is selfish because we put guys in a place where they have to fight not to think wrong thoughts. It is selfish because we draw attention to ourselves, taking the limelight away from others. When we are so full of the awareness of Jesus' love for us, we will not have the need to be in the limelight. We get the attention we need from the creator of the universe.

 PROTECT YOUR IMAGE

Don't think for one minute that just because we have to cover up, we can't be stylish. I have learned so much about fashion from my friend Shari Braendel, who wrote *Good Girls Don't Have to Dress Bad*. She shares that what we wear can be a distraction to what we are trying to say to others, including about our faith. We need to protect our opportunity to tell others about this radical love so their lives can be revolutionized as well!

It's not necessarily vain to dress stylish, have hair that is in, or know how to wear makeup that makes you look great. If we don't care about the way we look, we can be telling others "I don't feel valued" or "Don't pay attention to me; I'm not worth much."

THE 5 Bs OF BEAUTY

Rule #1 Be yourself. Dress in what you love and what loves you back.

Rule #2 Be colorful. Always wear shades that flatter you and your personality.

Rule #3 Be satisfied with your body. Wear the size that fits, not one too small.

Rule #4 Be beautiful. Remember you are amazing exactly as you are!

Rule #5 Be respectful. Ask yourself, "Would this outfit trip up a guy?"

—Shari Braendel,
Good Girls Don't Have to Dress Bad

It is often said that first impressions are the biggest impressions. Whether we like it or not, others will often judge us by what they see. These impressions can stick for a long time, and if they are not good ones, they are hard to overcome. What impression do we give others of Jesus, who lives in us?

Are the clothes you wear sending good messages such as "I know that I am valuable"? Or do they send negative messages such as "I need attention. Please look at me!"? What does the image you project say about you?

His Revolutionary Love

128

 # PROTECT THE TEMPLE

First Corinthians 6:19 tells us that our bodies are very valuable because our bodies are where God lives; we are his temple. I hope knowing this will help you want to take care of yourself. Our bodies need rest and not too much stress. We need to eat properly—not too much, not too little, and not a ton of garbage. We need to exercise to develop strong bones and to tone muscles.

Let's face it, life isn't easy. We all have our stressful moments. Some of us have really seriously hard stuff to deal with. We all have ways of getting through our days. Some people (like me) deal with stress by eating too much. Some people don't eat at all. Some fill their bodies with harmful substances or even cut themselves.

MY DIARY
November 2 (age nineteen): "I can tell that emotionally I'm going through a hard time because I want to eat all the time—even when I'm full!"

None of these methods heal our pain, only mask it. When we find ourselves wanting to destroy our temple rather than care for it, we really need to ask others who are mature in their faith to help us. These actions are outward symptoms that our hearts need healing. We need help from others to start that healing process and learn to protect our bodies instead.

We Protect Together

When a girl is in love, what does she usually do? She takes extra care to look nice and care for herself. You, my friend, are loved! I hope knowing just how crazy Jesus is about you will cause you to want to take care of yourself!

Like me, have you ever struggled with dealing with problems in unhealthy ways? How do you think remembering Jesus' love for you could change the way you look at your body?

# PROTECT THE GATE

Do Not Enter. I'm sure you've seen a sign like this before. Sometimes it's posted to protect something beyond a door or gate. Sometimes it's posted to protect us, the people outside the gate. Sometimes it's there for both.

Do Not Enter. I'm guessing you know what this means. It's a simple enough sign, but it seems like people get confused about it anyway. So here goes. You are not to be involved physically with anyone before marriage.

Not in any way. Not in any form.

If any behavior you engage in involves the parts of your body that are normally covered up, then it's sexual. If the behavior is with someone you are not married to, it's wrong. Guy, girl—doesn't matter. It's a no go area.

I know. It's hard. No, seriously, I KNOW. Every time I dated someone different, the temptation started again. The older I got, the worse the temptation became. But take it from someone who chose to listen to the sign—I never once wished that I had crossed this boundary.

> **T-SHIRTS FOR TEMPTATION**
> 1. Do Not Enter
> 2. See No Evil
> 3. Road Narrows
> 4. His Eyes Are Upon You
> 5. My Dad Has a Black Belt

I have, however, met many women who wished they never had. One young woman I knew put it this way: "*Imagine there's someone wandering around out there who, for the rest of your life, knows things about you, about your body and your heart, that no one should know except your husband. And this person doesn't love you—in fact, he may not even like you. Pretty disgusting, isn't it?"*

I was once given the advice, "If you wouldn't do it in front of your dad, don't do it." Father God is always there, right?

In Ephesians 4:26, 27, the Bible tells us to not give the devil a foothold. In other words, do not create opportunities for temptations and sin in our lives. We are to be alert for the enemy and the situations he will set up to cause us to sin. The temptations themselves will look different for each one of us, because he knows which ones work best on each person. Do you know what your weaknesses are?

Images that seem harmless are some of the things Satan may use to tempt us. Does the following scene sound familiar to you at all?

It had been a really stressful week and we just wanted to laugh. My friend and I checked the movies and chose one that the reviews said was "hilarious." It didn't start out too bad, but as the plot got deeper, so did the crude jokes and inappropriate scenes. My friend finally said, "I think we should walk out." So we did!

We need to protect our eyes. If we see impure images again and again, over time our vision can become clouded. Our hearts can become calloused. The things that once startled us or pricked our conscience no longer will. That's dangerous, because once our mind accepts images of sin as OK, it can be much easier for our actions to follow.

> *What temptations do you face that come through your eyes? Can you pinpoint the scenarios in your own life that Satan sets up to tempt you? What do they look like?*

So how do you prepare to stand up to this huge temptation? By protecting your heart. The writer of Psalm 119 revealed, "I have hidden your word in my heart that I might not sin against you" (v. 11). When we have his words filling our minds and our hearts, our actions will follow. We become what we think. We don't just wake up one day and decide to obey God or to sin. Obedience and sin both start with a thought, which is why we have to protect our minds.

In 2 Corinthians 10:4, 5, Paul told the Corinthians to make every thought obedient to Christ. That is definitely a very difficult thing to do, but if you will begin to pay close attention to your thoughts—not allowing yourself to dwell on those that are not pleasing to him—you will see huge changes in your heart and actions. The Bible is your God-tool to help you do just that.

> *The world is unprincipled. It's dog-eat-dog out there! The world doesn't fight fair. But we don't live or fight our battles that way—never have and never will. The tools of our trade aren't for marketing or manipulation, but they are for demolishing that entire massively corrupt culture. We use our powerful God-tools for smashing warped philosophies, tearing down barriers erected against the truth of God, fitting every loose thought and emotion and impulse into the structure of life shaped by Christ. Our tools are ready at hand for clearing the ground of every obstruction and building lives of obedience into maturity.*
>
> —2 Corinthians 10:3-6 (*The Message*)

What does Philippians 4:8 say that we should think on?

HE PROTECTS US

Sometimes our attempts to protect our heart and body fail, either because of our own choices or because someone crosses our boundaries against our wishes. In either case, we can ask Jesus to heal and/or forgive us. He can and will make us pure again. God may use many different things to bring healing: his Word, godly friends, prayer, a mentor, or counseling. Be open to them all— I was!

When I got out of high school, I went through a year of counseling. It was one of the best things that happened in my life. God used this time to lay a firm foundation in my mind and heart; I'm so glad that I went! I needed others to help me to get healed. Like me, you may need a little help getting healed too.

Don't beat yourself up if you feel like you have not protected your life and now it is a mess. One of the wonderful things about Jesus is that since he came to earth and lived a fully human life, he experienced all of the same things we experience. He experienced happiness, sorrow, love, betrayal, friendship, and temptation.

Maybe you thought Jesus would have no idea how you felt in a certain situation. Remember, his love is amazing—revolutionary! He doesn't just imagine he knows how you feel—he *actually knows*. We are reminded of this in his Word (Hebrews 4:14-16, *The Message*):

> *Now that we know what we have—Jesus, this great High Priest with ready access to God—let's not let it slip through our fingers. We don't have a priest who is out of touch with our reality. He's been through weakness and testing, experienced it all—all but the sin. So let's walk right*

up to him and get what he is so ready to give. Take the mercy, accept the help.

You can read about Jesus' one-on-one encounter with Satan in Matthew 4. You'll see that, when resisting the temptations Satan was throwing his way, Jesus quoted Scripture. Saying God's very words strengthened his own heart and made the enemy back down. Jesus reminded the devil that living for and honoring his father was the most important thing to him—and that was what he did.

> *No test or temptation that comes your way is beyond the course of what others have had to face. All you need to remember is that God will never let you down; he'll never let you be pushed past your limit; he'll always be there to help you come through it.*
> —1 Corinthians 10:13, *The Message*

If we are going to win the battles over temptation, we have to guard ourselves—our bodies, minds, hearts, eyes—and run to Jesus. When we do sin we need to ask for forgiveness so that the enemy does not have an opportunity to tempt us to cover it up. Jesus makes a promise to those who run to him: "'Because he loves me,' says the LORD, 'I will rescue him; I will protect him, for he acknowledges my name'" (Psalm 91:14).

I WILL PROTECT HIM, FOR HE ACKNOWLEDGES MY NAME.

Jesus has given us the tools that we need to overcome temptation and protect our hearts and minds: his Word, his love, his power, his strength, and other Christians who can pray and support us. Make the choice to overcome and take the steps to do it!

Connection

Make a connection with the one who wants you more than anything. Pray:

> *Jesus, I can see how it all comes together. Life isn't just a matter of those who are lucky and those who aren't. It is a whole lot more about choices. I want to make the right ones. Show me clearly the steps I need to take today to protect my heart and my mind. Amen.*

Radical Pursuits

Share with a trustworthy Christian leader or friend a temptation that you are struggling with. Often, being honest and sharing takes much of the strength out of the temptation. Ask her to pray for you every day and to check with you regularly to see how you are doing with leaning on Jesus for his strength to overcome whatever your weaknesses are.

We Protect Together

CHAPTER ~ 8

We Relate Together

*"There is a time for everything,
and a season for every activity
under the heavens: . . .
a time to embrace and
a time to refrain from embracing,
a time to search and a time to give up."*

—Ecclesiastes 3:1, 5, 6

I'll try one more time, I thought to myself as I slipped the note onto his windshield. I knew he had moved on. Kim told me Greg had a new girlfriend, but I didn't want to believe it. Just two days ago he had sent me flowers saying, "I hope you like your new school." Surely that meant we were more than friends.

Wait. Let me go back and start at the beginning.

Greg and I first met in junior high. I sang a solo in church one Sunday. After the performance he called me and that was all it took. There is just something about having someone like you *first*! Even more exciting was the fact that he was an older guy. Since we went to different schools and couldn't drive, the attraction quickly fizzled. The phone calls dwindled to just a couple of times and life returned to normal.

At least it did for Greg. For me, he was not going to be one of those guys I got over. All through junior high I wrote his name all over my notebooks.

In ninth grade, my chance finally came. Our church was having a Valentine's get-together and Greg asked me. I was out of my mind! A junior now, he was a huge weight lifter (6'2", 250 pounds) and captain of the football team. His smile grabbed me. My parents let me go to the celebration, but since I wasn't sixteen yet, I still wasn't allowed to date. Once again, the phone calls stopped.

Finally, I turned sixteen, and with my birthday came a huge decision. Leaving the Christian school where I attended junior high, I transitioned to the public high school just two blocks from home. I had mixed motives for my decision. Our youth pastor often encouraged us to share our faith. Well, I didn't have any friends who didn't know Jesus! So I decided it was time to get some. Motive number two was Greg—Cedar Falls High School was his school. OK, now we are caught up to the note and the flowers I received from him days before my first day of tenth grade.

All summer I had been contacting Greg. I'd call him "just to chat." We were friends, right? I'd leave him notes on his car at his job. Drive by his house. I gave any excuse to make my reason to contact him seem legit. (OK, OK, in print this looks pretty creepy. Even stalkerish. But don't tell me you don't do the same kind of thing on Facebook! How much time have you spent perusing that one guy's page lately?)

HE'S JUST NOT THAT INTO ME

I was missing something huge (or maybe I was just ignoring the obvious). Greg was friendly, but he never initiated anything. He was a good guy; he just didn't want to go out with me. I wouldn't accept that he just wasn't that into me! The flowers were a nice way of saying "Hey, I know you are going to be new at the school. I hope it goes good for you." But I wanted it to be SO much more than that.

My sophomore year was my worst. Greg's locker was on the same floor as mine, so I would see him at least once a day. Absolute torture! Even worse, his new girlfriend was a good friend of my good friend, Kim. Even though she was very nice, it was so hard not to be jealous of her! When she showed me a ring Greg had given her, my heart broke.

WHAT WAS WRONG WITH ME?

I didn't do such a great job of controlling my thoughts; I let it get to me. I remember sitting at home one weekend night, emo-type stuff pouring out of my speakers, me crying my brains out. *Why doesn't he like me?! What's wrong with me??* (Have any of you been there? Not a pretty place, is it?)

Looking back now, it's all a whole lot clearer. There wasn't anything wrong with me. Greg didn't want to be chased. Greg didn't want a girl who would constantly contact him. Greg didn't want a girl writing notes to him. And at that time, Greg didn't want a girl who was all that into Jesus.

I finally got it. I quit trying to manipulate my relationships and started trusting God. When Greg was a junior in college, things changed. He did want a girl who would write verses to him—a girl mature in her faith. He finally chased *me.*

At that time, I was at the training school I've mentioned. I shared with my counselor how the guy I had liked *forever* (seven years, actually) finally liked me! He had called me at school, saying he was coming for spring break to see me. I was crazy excited. My counselor then reminded me I had made a commitment to not date while I was at school. My commitment was to give 100 percent of my heart and attention to Jesus. Gently, she pointed out it is impossible to give your all to two relationships at the same time. (It wouldn't be your all then, would it?)

I knew she was right, but I did NOT want to hear THAT! I called Greg and told him that I couldn't have a relationship with him. It ripped my heart out!

Seven months later, with school out, I went home to visit my parents. Guess who was at church? Greg. At this point, I knew that God was giving me the OK to say yes. We started dating and were married a year later. And I have been sending him verses ever since.

# IN HIS TIME

"Man's rejection equals God's protection." If you had told me that when I was in high school, I would have screamed! I was so over man's rejection. I didn't like not having a boyfriend. I only got asked out by guys who didn't live the way I did. I felt lonely; my friends were dating. Yet as I look at the big picture now, I am incredibly grateful for God's wisdom.

As much as I didn't like it, it's true: man's rejection is God's protection. If Greg and I had started dating when we were younger, we probably would not have made it. We probably would not have overcome the temptation to have sex before we got married (it was hard enough waiting from the time we starting dating until we said "I do!"). Not waiting would have ruined our relationship.

So, you might be wondering, what's my point? Wait seven years for a guy and then it will happen? Chase a guy like crazy and he'll run away?

Well, kind of. My point is, there is a time for everything. You need to be patient. You need to pray. And you need to keep trusting in God's wisdom for your life.

You also need to be honest with yourself. I wasn't always so good at that, as you can see. But if a guy likes you, he'll let you know. If he doesn't approach you, he's either just not that into you or he has issues with confidence and courage. And if the latter is his problem, then he needs to get those on his own. You can't do it for him, and you can't make him like you. It may seem harsh, but I think it is true. But don't just take *my* word for it.

Drew, age fifteen, told me, " *When I like a girl, I'll befriend her, talk to her a lot, and pay more attention to her.*"

Kevin, age eighteen, answered the question "Is it hard to take the initiative in a relationship?" He said, " *No way! If the guy doesn't take initiative, the girl shouldn't be with the guy.*"

When it comes to waiting for a guy to take the initiative, do you have a problem with that? Why? While you are waiting, what kinds of things could you do that would make you more ready to date?

Don't get me wrong; I'm not saying you can't talk to a guy. Go ahead, start the conversation. In fact, talking first can help to take the pressure off the shy guy. But at some point, you've got to let him take the next step.

Often it seemed like my relationships got stuck in the Friendship Zone (insert spooky music here). Have you been there? You want there to be more (or you think *he* wants there to be more), but you just aren't sure. What are you supposed to do when you are stuck?

Wait. If he likes you, he'll let you know. There is nothing worse than saying it first and being wrong! Once those words have come out, it's like trying to put toothpaste back in the tube when you have squeezed out too much! As hard as it is, enjoy the Friendship Zone while you are in it. There are a lot of great things there. You can learn how to communicate better with a guy. You can figure out how they think. Work on learning to give and take in a relationship.

Remember, once you start going out, there is no going back. The relationship changes. This weird thing happens where there is pressure to act a certain way. From that point, there are only two ways that a dating relationship ends—just two. You either get married or you break up. If you break up, chances are you won't be able to get back to the great friendship that you started with. It's

5 SIGNS YOU'RE IN THE FRIENDSHIP ZONE

1. His nickname for you is "Sis."
2. He signs off all his messages with "Your FRIEND."
3. He never answers your texts on Friday or Saturday nights.
4. He gave you new athletic socks for your birthday.
5. You have a great friend, who happens to be a guy.

just too hard and too weird. So don't rush into anything. God tells us there is a time for everything, and a purpose for everything. Take your time. Find out your purpose.

PLAY IT OUT

Maybe you aren't dating yet, or don't even want to be. Still, there's stuff in this chapter you might want to think through. It can be really helpful to play out situations in your head. You can think about how you would handle them should those circumstances ever happen to you. And even if you aren't the one dating, maybe you'll be able to help a friend with her romantic troubles!

Scenario #1: You are sitting in biology when you get a text (assuming you are even allowed to have cell phones in class). Peeking under your desk, you see the text is from a guy—a guy who just so happens to be sitting two rows in front of you. "Plans tmro pm? Wanna see a movie?"

DON'T MESS UP YOUR HEART; DON'T MESS WITH YOUR MIND.

This guy is cute; really cute! Any girl in that room would have loved receiving that text. But, you've heard stuff about him from pretty believable sources—heard what he does with his dates and what he does at parties. What are you going to do? He's right there! Looking at you; reading your expression.

Friend, the way I see it, you have one option—you've got to say "SRY but THX" (or something like that). Get plans with someone else if you have to, so you won't be tempted. But if you already know that this guy isn't a Christ follower, the wise decision is to say no up front. Don't mess up your heart; don't mess with your mind. Or his, for that matter. Protect them.

If you're feeling really brave, you could even catch him in the hall and just say: "Look, I'm a Christian, and I'm just trying to do the right thing. I like you, but I've heard you're into doing things that I'm just not comfortable with, so that's why I said no." Or you could just wait until your church had their next youth event and invite him to come. Better yet, get a guy friend to invite him.

I know—pretty weird, right? But that's the point. You're loved by a radical guy, and his revolutionary love can empower you to do some really amazing things. Like saying no to a guy every girl has a crush on. Or even sharing your faith. Will this be hard? You bet! Will you wish with all your heart that you could just take the easy road? Probably, at least sometimes. But you have to trust me here (and if you can't trust me, trust Jesus): down the road you will be one very happy girl about your decision to follow Christ.

Scenario #2: You are sitting in biology when you get a text. Peeking under your desk, you see the text is from a guy: "Plans tmro pm? Wanna see a movie?" This time, you are not quite positive, but you think this guy might be a Christian. You heard from a friend that he goes to church—is even a part of his youth group. You are so excited; you text right back without learning more about him: "Snds great!"

Friday night comes around. Bad sign #1: he asks you to meet him at his house. He needs to be man enough to come to your house to pick you up and meet your parents. Old fashioned? Yep, but what type of guy do you want anyway? One who treats you like a queen or one who treats you like every other girl?

Although at least, if you have your own car, you also have your own way out. So let's say you go ahead and meet him there. But when you get there, bad sign #2: "Hey, my parents are out, so how about if we just pick up a movie and watch it at my house?" What? Go to his house? His parents aren't there? Time to get out—fast! Tell him you have other plans, and go get some. Tell him you aren't OK with being at his house for a date. Tell him your parents will ask you to give a complete review of the latest release. Tell him whatever—just get out of there.

But let's say you don't. He loads the movie, grabs a blanket, and pulls you onto the couch. Bad sign #3: Ummm, do I really need to spell these out for you anymore?

The Bible says in 1 Corinthians 10:13 that God will provide a way of escape from temptation. In this scenario, he's already provided you at least two. But he's not going to make the choices for you. You've got to decide what is the best thing for you to do.

 ## HE WALKS WITH US

In his letters to the Corinthians, Paul wrote quite a bit about right relationships between people and between believers and Jesus. Read the whole letter some time when you have a chance—there's a lot of good stuff in it! In 2 Corinthians 6:16 Paul reminded people that "we are the temple of the living God. As God has said: 'I will live with them and walk among them, and I will be their God, and they will be my people.'" Then he continued in chapter 7:1: "Therefore, since we have these promises, dear friends, let us purify ourselves from everything that contaminates body and spirit, perfecting holiness out of reverence for God."

"We are the temple of the living God." Isn't that amazingly awesome? Once you have accepted Christ into your life, he lives *in* you. He walks with you. He relates with you.

Knowing this should give you strength and courage—just what you need to make some of the hard choices that will get you through the sticky situations you might encounter in your dating life.

Knowing this should also fill you up inside. Remember Lexi and Zoe's story of needing to be filled up? No matter what your dating status, remember that guys were never meant to fill up our hearts. In fact, when we look to them to do that, they often feel smothered. To keep the interest fresh, you have to hold a little bit back; keep a little mystery about yourself. Don't dump all of your heart and mind at once. They don't have the maturity to handle it, and keeping bits of yourself secret protects your heart as well.

I WILL LIVE WITH THEM AND WALK AMONG THEM, AND I WILL BE THEIR GOD, AND THEY WILL BE MY PEOPLE.

If you're feeling the need to dump, why not go to your best friend, your revolutionary lover, and give it all to him? Jesus loves being smothered. He is excited for you to tell him just how great he is and how much you love him too! He loves smothering you back as well. He said, "If anyone thirsts, let him come to me and drink. Rivers of living water will brim and spill out of the depths of anyone who believes in me this way, just as the Scripture says"

(John 7:38, *The Message*). He is just waiting for you to come so he can tell you how beautiful and priceless you are.

Connection

Make a connection with the one who wants you more than anything. Pray:

Jesus, I want to be wanted! Thank you that you already want me. Help me to come to you when I have feelings for a guy creeping up in my heart. Help me to trust you to bring the guy you want in my life when it is the perfect time. I am so glad that I can trust you. Amen.

Radical Pursuits

Write out a game plan—a plan for how you will respond and what you will do when you are attracted to a guy. The time to have a plan is now, not when you are under pressure. How will you honor God? How will you protect your heart when it comes to guys?

Write out your game plan here.

CHAPTER ~ 9

We Love Together

"Two are better than one."

—Ecclesiastes 4:9

Over it already. That is how Chelsea felt about her friendship with Kate. At first their friendship was so exciting! They had a lot in common: both were athletes, both didn't worry about fashion, both hated girl drama. That was last year. This year things were different.

It started when Kate got her first boyfriend; it was almost as if she thought she was now better than Chelsea. She began forwarding every text she got from a boy. What was Chelsea supposed to do with that? She didn't know what to do. Were they just going in different directions?

Girlfriends! Our relationships with friends can be almost as complicated, if not more so, as those with boys! A lot of time and energy can be used trying to figure out how friendships are supposed to work, or trying to repair the damage when they don't work out right.

THERE IS ONLY ONE THING WORTH BEING CONCERNED ABOUT.

Jesus had lots of friends when he was here on earth. We can look to his revolutionary love for an example of how to treat our friends. He demonstrated his nothing-held-back love with some very special friends, Mary and Martha. We can learn so much from their intimate bond.

We get our first glimpse into this unique friendship in Luke 10:38-42. Jesus and his disciples were passing through Mary and Martha's village. Martha welcomed Jesus into her home. While speaking, Jesus immediately captured Mary's heart. She sat at his feet, hanging on every word he said. Meanwhile, Martha was distracted, preparing for the big dinner. She became irritated with Mary, who was just sitting while Martha did all the work. "Lord, don't you care that my sister has left me to do the work by myself? Tell her to help me!" she begged. (Sounds like something I might hear at my house!)

Jesus gave a surprising answer. In the kindest way, he addressed Martha: "My dear Martha, you are worried and upset over all these details! There is only one thing worth being concerned about. Mary has discovered it, and it will not be taken away from her" (Luke 10:41, 42, *NLT*). In this glimpse into his relationship with Mary and Martha, Jesus demonstrated true friendship to both of them. He protected and supported Mary and offered advice and encouragement to Martha.

 ## LOVE IS TRUSTWORTHY

Jesus knew Mary; he knew her heart and her motives. Unlike me, who would be willing to do just about anything to get out of kitchen work, Mary was genuinely captivated by Jesus. Jesus recognized love when he saw it. He sensed that Mary wanted to learn anything and everything she could about him; she was completely mesmerized by the truth he was speaking. She was exactly where Jesus wanted her to be—taking it all in. He commended her for making the best decision.

This wasn't the only time Jesus had to stand up for Mary. In John 12:1-11, Jesus was again eating dinner with his favorite family. Martha was serving, but this time Mary wasn't just a bystander. She made a decision that would cause others to remember her for as long as there is time. Mary took the thing most precious to her, expensive perfume valued at over a year's worth of work, and poured it onto Jesus' feet! Next, she took her hair and wiped the fragrant oil into his dry, cracked skin.

INTENSE LOVE DOES NOT MEASURE, IT JUST GIVES.

—Mother Teresa

Judas didn't like her actions. The dude on the list of world's worst friends blurted out: "That perfume was worth a year's wages. It should have been sold and the money given to the poor." Didn't he appear to be the holy one? In reality, he didn't care all that much for the poor; he was the treasurer and known for stealing.

Jesus stood up to Judas on behalf of his precious friend, Mary. "Leave her alone." He was not afraid to support his friend, even when others did not. He knew Mary's heart and treasured her.

He wouldn't allow others to take her down.

> *Have you ever been in a situation where you were faced with a decision to stand up for a friend or join in with others making fun of her? How did you react?*

His Revolutionary Love

By standing up for Mary, Jesus demonstrated that he is trustworthy. A trustworthy person is someone you feel safe with. You are secure sharing your heart.

How do you find a friend like that? When looking for someone you feel completely safe with and can rely on, ask a few questions:

- *What does she talk about?*
- *How does she spend most of her free time?*
- *Does she often find fault and judge others or does she protect her friends?*
- *Does she speak highly of other friends or does she put others down so she can look better?*
- *Does she look for ways she can encourage other people?*

It can be hard to ask these tough questions, especially if this is a new friendship that seems really fun. But know this: if your new friend speaks unkindly about others, you can be sure at some point she'll do the same to you! The Bible says this about these types of friends:

- *"Mean people spread mean gossip; their words smart and burn" (Proverbs 16:27, The Message).*
- *"A perverse person stirs up conflict, and a gossip separates close friends" (Proverbs 16:28).*
- *"The words of a gossip are like choice morsels; they go down to the inmost parts" (Proverbs 18:8).*
- *"Gossips can't keep secrets, so never confide in blabbermouths" (Proverbs 20:19, The Message).*

Do you find it easy to get caught in the middle of conversations about others that are unkind? If so, how can you get out of these? How can understanding Jesus' radical love for you help you change the way you speak about others?

A conversation in which another person is put down seems like no big deal. That person doesn't know anyway, right? But you know exactly what happens. Eventually those words wind their way back to the person. Gossip damages people. It doesn't even matter if what is said is true or not. Being talked about in an unkind way tears a person down. We need to remember Jesus died for that person we are talking about. If she is a Christ follower, we need to protect her as our sister in Christ. Follower or not, we need to love her.

Satan always uses gossip to hurt. And possibly the person who gossip hurts the most is the person who speaks it. Just think about it. If you're one of those people spreading rumors about others, why should anyone trust you with a secret? And what if you do get a piece of information about someone, and you pass it along, and it's completely wrong? Then, you've not only hurt someone else, you also look like a fool for believing it in the first place.

But that's not the worst thing. The real problem is that every time you say yes to gossip, you allow your heart to become a little more calloused. You say no to caring for others. It makes it that much easier for you to not just say bad things about others, but to actually *do* harmful things to others.

WHAT A PERSON PLANTS, HE WILL HARVEST.
— Galatians 6:7,
The Message

We've read the Bible verse about guarding your heart before. But it is interesting to see what advice directly follows that verse: "Keep vigilant watch over your heart; that's where life starts. Don't talk out of both sides of your mouth; avoid careless banter, white lies, and gossip" (Proverbs 4:23, 24, *The Message*).

What does Galatians 6:7 say will happen to those who sow seeds of gossip?

Once we figure out who's trustworthy, we need to pick a couple of people we would think of as our truest friends—those we can truly confide in. My mother used to tell me, "If you have one or two close friends, you are blessed." One or two? Why so few? I wanted more like ten or twelve, or at the very least seven—one for every day of the week! Proverbs 18:24 leads me to believe that my mom was on to something: "One who has unreliable friends soon comes to ruin, but there is a friend who sticks closer than a brother" (Proverbs 18:24). It's hard to have lots of friends who are all equally trustworthy. Make sure the ones closest to you are ones who are as loyal as sisters—or more so!

> ### 5 TRUE FRIENDSHIPS
> 1. Anne of Green Gables and Diana
> 2. David and Jonathan
> 3. Batman and Robin
> 4. Harry Potter, Ron Weasley, and Hermione Granger
> 5. Frodo and Sam

A note of warning: Sometimes you may feel close to a person very quickly—this happens a lot in places like church camp or a sleepover. Large amounts of unhurried time are a great way to build up relationships, but you may be tempted to open up with those you don't know well. Be cautious—if you haven't known these friends very long, your secrets could become the hot topic in school on Monday.

His Revolutionary Love

 # LOVE TELLS THE TRUTH

Have you ever had a friend who would tell you the truth when you asked how your hair looked? a friend who gave you a heads-up when you had green stuff stuck between your teeth? That's a good friend!

Good friends tell the truth, like Jesus did. When Martha put Mary down, Jesus didn't turn around and put Martha down. In a loving way, he told her the truth about her actions so that she wouldn't continue in a destructive way. That's revolutionary love in action. Proverbs 27:6 tells us that wounds from a sincere friend are better than many kisses from an enemy. It's not always easy being honest—pretending is much easier. But a true friend is truthful.

Ephesians 4:15 says we are to speak the truth in love. We just have to be sure that our motivation *is* love. I had a friend who would recklessly point out my faults, leaving me feeling wounded and hurt. At the end of the conversation she would say, "I'm just speaking the truth in love." Speaking the truth, maybe. Loving me, no.

When you see something in your friend's life that is not best for them, what do you do? How do you deliver the truth?

We Love Together

When we share the same goal with a friend—to know Christ more intimately and become like him—we can use our words and

> As iron sharpens iron,
> so one person
> sharpens another.
> —Proverbs 27:17

actions to sharpen one another, to make each other better people. Sometimes the words that a friend may share are words we do not want to hear. The truth is often hard to hear. That friend may even be an adult. Remember, our true friends love us and want God's best for us. They won't let us keep doing things that will ultimately hurt us. "Better is open rebuke than hidden love" (Proverbs 27:5).

LOVE SEES THE BIG PICTURE

Girl drama! Doesn't it always come at the wrong time? Elizabeth was so excited! She had just been voted captain of the volleyball team. The next thing she knew, another team member was crying! Fueled by jealousy, the crying player attempted to create division because she wanted to be captain. Elizabeth didn't know what to do. This was supposed to be a happy time. It took a hug and calming words from her coach to help bring perspective to the whole situation.

I see Jesus did just that in his relationship with Martha; he helped her see the big picture. The urgent, such as getting dinner ready for guests, was important to her. But her practical priorities caused her to miss the most important thing: the Son of God sitting in her home. Jesus pointed out to her that some things in life are passing; some are forever.

Jesus helped his friends see the big picture on more than one occasion. Mary and Martha had a brother named Lazarus, whom

His Revolutionary Love

Jesus loved as well. In John 11, Lazarus became deathly sick. The women knew Jesus could heal him, so they sent a message to Jesus, telling him of Lazarus's sickness. They expected him to come as soon as possible to heal the friend he loved.

But he didn't come right away. During the wait, Lazarus died. Then Jesus told his disciples they were going to go back to where Lazarus lived with Martha and Mary. "Lazarus is dead, and for your sake I am glad I was not there, so that you may believe. But let us go to him" (John 11:14, 15).

When he arrived, Martha went right up to him—you can see she felt completely comfortable talking to her friend and showing her grief. "If you had been here, my brother would not have died. But even now I know that God will give you whatever you ask."

Have you ever been face-to-face with a friend who is in real trouble, a friend who is deeply sad? It's not an easy situation. What do you do? What do you say?

As a fourth grader, I wasn't too mature. Maybe lots of fourth graders are immature, but I'm sure I could have handled the situation differently. It was Friday night—homecoming, to be exact. All day in school we had chatted up going to the high school football game. I couldn't wait! There was just one catch. In order for me to go and sit in the stands without my parents, my best friend had to go along with me. That was the only way my parents would say yes.

My friend was supposed to call and let me know. After school I waited and waited, but she never called. Finally, I called her. "Hi!" I said excitedly.

"Lynn, my dad died today."

Silent. I was just silent. I didn't know what to say. I had no idea what to do!

Finally, I blurted out, "Can you still go to the game?" Once those terrible words slipped out, I knew I blew it. I just had no idea what to do for my friend.

Here's a story of someone who *did* have a clue. Alexandra's dad was moving out. Moving out? How could he do that? But that is exactly what he had told her. She shared these painful words with her best friend, Madi. What did Madi do?

She listened. Though she didn't know what it was like exactly to have that kind of pain in her family, she let Alexandra talk. She let Alexandra cry. She was there for her friend.

A couple of years later, it was Madi who had hurt in her family. And do you know who was there? Alexandra. You see, Alexandra knew pain and she knew how to be a friend to Madi, who was hurting.

Like Alexandra, Jesus didn't just observe the pain that his friends were experiencing. He got involved; he got down in the dirt with them. That's what radical love does.

Jesus saw the grief of Martha, and later, Mary's tears, and those of their friends. Jesus didn't back away. He didn't look for an excuse to avoid being around them while they were weeping. Instead, he wept with them. He was so moved by compassion for his friends, Jesus cried too.

But then he did what he had come to do. "Did I not tell you that if you believe, you will see the glory of God?" Jesus said to Martha. He was trying to get her to see the bigger picture. Jesus headed down to the tomb, called Lazarus out of the grave, and brought him back to life. In the end many believed in Jesus and told others of this miracle.

A GREAT FRIEND HELPS YOU SEE THE BIG PICTURE.

Like Jesus, a great friend comes alongside you, empathizes with you, but doesn't just stop there. A great friend helps you to see the big picture—God's picture. Maybe you have a friend who's injured, causing her to miss her favorite sports season. Maybe your best bud wasn't invited to a huge party and now she feels like a loser. A true friend comes alongside and lovingly points how God might be behind it all. He could possibly be at work so that he can receive glory and others will see his love.

And even if you don't have the answers, or can't see the big picture yourself, you can be there for your friend and pray together for understanding. Radical love looks beyond the obvious and in faith encourages a friend to believe Jesus will bring about the best in her life.

When have you been a cheerleader to a friend, helping her to see how a bad situation could turn out for good?

A godly friend will help you see the big picture beyond today's temptation and how it could affect tomorrow. Keep yourself in a place where you are accountable to others (parents, godly friends, youth pastors, etc.). They can help you overcome temptation. Sometimes they can see a situation much clearer because they are on the outside. A fresh perspective may be just what you need to come out of your trial the winner.

> *Two are better than one, because they have a good return for their work; if one falls down, his friend can help him up. But pity the man who falls and has no one to help him up! Also, if two lie down together, they will keep warm. But how can one keep warm alone? Though one may be overpowered, two can defend themselves. A cord of three strands is not quickly broken.*
> —Ecclesiastes 4:9-12

 OUR RESPONSE TO LOVE

Mary knew the love that Jesus had for her. She knew it, and it compelled her to respond. Earlier, we looked at her response: pouring out her best, the most expensive thing that she owned. She humbled herself and gave all she had.

I hope that after the time we've spent together in *His Revolutionary Love* that you, like Mary, feel compelled to respond to his love. My prayer for you is that you will sit at his feet like Mary, for the rest of your life—hanging on his every word and knowing that he is speaking to you, wanting you, pursuing you, hoping for you, and loving you. I hope that you have soaked in the truth of this amazing, life-changing love and that you will never be the same.

 ## *Connection*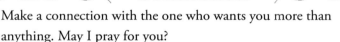

Make a connection with the one who wants you more than anything. May I pray for you?

> *Jesus, love of our lives, this has been an amazing journey. Seeing firsthand that the creator of the universe is crazy for us is really beyond what we can comprehend. Jesus, may this be the beginning for my friend. I pray she would sense the Holy Spirit close to her in the days and years to come, and her heart will forever be one with yours. Thank-you is not enough for all that you are and all you have given us. May our lives reflect hearts that are saturated with love; may we honor you as our gift in return. May this be our worship. Amen.*

We Love Together

Radical Pursuits

When Jesus' love fills you up, it can't help but spill out into your world. Think about how his revolutionary love can make a difference in your life.

Be radical in your friendships:

- Write a note to someone who's going through a hard time.
- Just sit and listen to someone who is sad.
- If you know someone who needs a dose of truth, find a way to say it with love.

Be radical in your romances:

- Always remember to put Jesus first.
- Don't rush into anything; be patient.
- Treat any guys you date with the respect and care that you'd want them to give to you.

Be radical all over!

- Look out for people who need Jesus' love. Don't be afraid to talk to people who are different, or lonely, or suffering.
- Be different. Be the one people can trust. Stop gossip in its tracks. Be honest.
- Run to Jesus for your completion. Read his love notes to you every day. Get filled up in him, then tell someone about it!

His Revolutionary Love

ACKNOWLEDGMENTS

To my Jesus: Thank you so much for capturing my heart when I was young. You have given me love and purpose that this life could never have offered. This book is my attempt at making you famous.

To Greg: Thank you for believing in me when I didn't. You started telling me early in our marriage "You should write a book," but I didn't believe. Your support goes above anything I could ever ask for. I love you so much!

To Zach, Mariah, and Madi: Thank you for embracing a mom that has been crazy for Jesus your whole life. May you always know that he is wild about you and in exchange for everything, offers you his very best.

To Mom: For introducing me to Jesus as a little girl, I will be forever grateful. You're the best!

To my Martin and Cowell family: Thank you for all the prayers and words of encouragement. A big family is the best!

To Julie: Thanks for being a friend for all time. For helping me invest in girls, reading my writings, and giving out hugs after each rejection, I am so grateful! Thank you for helping me not give up!

To the staff and ministry teams of Proverbs 31 Ministries:
As Marybeth said first, "I love doing life with you!" You are an amazing group of women that I am honored and proud to minister with. LeAnn, Lysa, and Renee, thank you for your unselfish leadership.

To all the girls I have mentored through L.I.G.H.T. and RadRev Girls and my blog, especially the first L.I.G.H.T. group who went through my study—Cassie, Gretchen, Jo, Katelynn, Kelly, Laurali, Megan, and Rachel. Thanks for letting me be a part of your lives!

To Blythe Daniel: You believed that this was a message that needed to be heard. Thanks for taking the risk on me!

To Bob, Laura, Sarah, and Lindsay and the rest of the Standard Publishing team: Each one of you "got" me and the message of this book. Thank you so much for your efforts and support.

THE AUTHOR

Lynn Cowell and her husband, Greg, have three teens: Zach, Mariah, and Madi. A perfect day for their family involves hiking boots, well-worn sweatshirts, and anything combining chocolate and peanut butter.

As an author and speaker with Proverbs 31 Ministries, Lynn's greatest passion is leading teens and their moms to find what every heart truly wants: completion in Christ. She does this through her site for teens at www.RadRevolution.org and for women at www.LynnCowell.com. Lynn writes for *Susie Magazine*, Focus on the Family, *Proverbs 31 Woman* and *Enrichment Journal*, as well as devotions for the Proverbs 31 "Encouragement for Today," which reaches hundreds of thousands of women daily. She also speaks around the country at conferences for girls and women—pouring out God's truth of how crazy he is for them.

Lynn has been mentoring girls for over nine years in small groups just like the ones she talked about in *His Revolutionary Love*. It was out of these wonderful experiences that the desire for this book was born.

BLOG: Dialog with Lynn through her blog, see pictures of her family, and follow her speaking schedule. She'd love to meet you at an event in your area! www.LynnCowell.com.

BOOKING LYNN TO SPEAK: If you are interested in booking Lynn for a speaking engagement, contact Proverbs 31 Ministries at speaker@proverbs31.org.

ABOUT PROVERBS 31 MINISTRIES

If you were inspired by *His Revolutionary Love* and want to deepen your own personal relationship with Jesus Christ, I encourage you to connect with Proverbs 31 Ministries. Proverbs 31 Ministries exists to be a trusted friend who will take you by the hand and walk by your side, no matter what your age! We help lead you one step closer to the heart of God through:

- Encouragement for Today, online daily devotions
- The P31 Woman monthly magazine
- Daily radio program
- Books and resources
- Dynamic speakers with life-changing messages
- Online communities
- Gather and Grow groups

If you are a teen, check out www.RadRevolution.org. You'll find inspirational entries, vlogs, conference information, RadRev groups, and fun tips on fashion too!

Maybe you're past that stage; you're a twenty-something. Check out our ministry just for you at www.SheSeeks.org.

To learn more about Proverbs 31 Ministries or to inquire about having Lynn Cowell speak at your event, call 877-731-4663 or visit www.proverbs31.org.

Proverbs 31 Ministries
616-G Matthews-Mint Hill Road • Matthews, NC 28105 • www.Proverbs31.org

Additional Resources You Will Love!

Secrets About Guys
Item #23329

Seduced by Sex : Saved by Love
Item #23964

Princess Unaware
Item #24340

So Much More Than Sexy
Item #24341

VISIT YOUR LOCAL CHRISTIAN BOOKSTORE
OR WWW.STANDARDPUB.COM

LEADER'S GUIDE

 **FREE RESOURCES**

Want to lead a group of girls through *His Revolutionary Love* but unsure where to start? Want to start your own RadRev group?

Go to either of the websites listed below to download a **free** leader's guide for *His Revolutionary Love: Jesus' Radical Pursuit of You.* You'll find:

- tons of small group tips, including how to mentor girls, troubleshoot, schedule meetings, and a lot more
- ideas for keeping it fun: icebreakers, special events you can hold, and activities of all sorts
- discussion questions and suggested memory verses for each chapter

Start a radical pursuit right now! Go to:

WWW.LYNNCOWELL.COM

OR

WWW.STANDARDPUB.COM/HISREVOLUTIONARYLOVE